Sleep Better

Jerome Palazzolo

CONTENTS

The author   i

Preface   1

Foreword   7

I.   To understand sleep and insomnia   11

II.   To understand the kind of insomniac you are   27

III.   Practical advices to spend a good night   55

Conclusion   79

Appendix   81

To know more…   99

… And even more   101

Useful addresses   103

THE AUTHOR

Jérôme Palazzolo is psychiatrist in Nice (France), part-time lecturer at the University of Nice - Sophia Antipolis and professor of Health Psychology at the International Senghor University of Alexandria (Egypt). Specialized in Psychopharmacology and Cognitivo-behavioural Therapy, he is the author of many reference articles as well as several works treating various psychiatric practices :

- *Words of pain.* America Star Books, Frederick (USA), 2015
- *Les troubles de la personnalité.* Mon Petit Éditeur (Groupe Publibook - Petit Futé), Paris, 2014
- *Les thérapies brèves - Actualités et perspectives des TCC.* Mon Petit Éditeur (Groupe Publibook - Petit Futé), Paris, 2013
- *L'homosexualité en Afrique - Regard anthropologique et psychologique.* Riveneuve, Paris, 2013
- *Sentiment de contrôle et gestion du stress – Une psychologie cognitive de la performance.* Retz, Paris, 2013
- *Risques et plongée - Actualités et perspectives.* Turtle Prod Edition, Hyères, 2013
- *Aidez vos proches à sortir de la toxicomanie et des addictions.* Mon Petit Editeur (Groupe Publibook - Petit Futé), Paris, 2012
- *Aidez vos proches à surmonter la dépression. Edition révisée.* Mon Petit Editeur (Groupe Publibook - Petit Futé), Paris, 2012
- *Cas cliniques en thérapies comportementales et cognitives. 3ème édition.* Elsevier-Masson, Collection Pratiques en Psychothérapie, Paris, 2012

- *Conscience et représentation de la maladie mentale et neurologique.* Mon Petit Éditeur (Groupe Publibook - Petit Futé), Paris, 2011
- *Strategies and methods for a fast recovery - A cognitive behavioral therapy manual.* Lambert Academic Publishing Editions, Londres (Royaume-Uni), 2010
- *La gestion du stress et de l'aquaphobie par les TCC - L'apport de la plongée sous-marine.* Mon Petit Éditeur (Groupe Publibook - Petit Futé), Paris, 2010
- *Sida et séropositivité : entre observance et adhésion - Un regard anthropologique en Francophonie.* Éditions Universitaires Européennes, Sarrebruck (Allemagne), 2010
- *Guide de l'urgence psychiatrique.* Med-Line, Paris, 2009
- *L'épreuve de la maladie organique - Un regard anthropologique.* Ellébore, Collection Champs Ouverts, Paris, 2009
- *Tabagisme - Plaisir et dépendance. Données actuelles et perspectives.* Hermann, Paris, 2009
- *Petite histoire de la masturbation.* Odile Jacob, Paris, 2009
- *Les exclus de la cité - Regard anthropologique et psychopathologique sur les enfants des rues.* Riveneuve, Paris, 2008
- *Coachez votre vie.* Odile Jacob, Paris, 2007
- *Dépression et anxiété - Mieux les comprendre pour mieux les prendre en charge.* Masson, Collection Abrégés de Médecine, Paris, 2007
- *Les thérapies comportementales et cognitives - Manuel pratique.* Editions In Press, Paris, 2007
- *La parole et l'écoute - La relation soignant-soigné face à l'épreuve du SIDA.* Ellébore, Collection Champs Ouverts, Paris, 2007
- *En finir avec l'insomnie.* Hachette Pratique, Paris, 2006
- *Aidez vos proches à surmonter la dépression.* Hachette Pratique, Paris, 2006
- *Aidez vos proches à surmonter l'alcoolisme.* Hachette Pratique, Paris, 2006
- *Le cannabis en question.* Hachette Pratique, Paris, 2006
- *Schizophrénie : l'annonce du diagnostic.* Editions In Press, Paris, 2006
- *Vieillissement, trouble bipolaire et schizophrénie.* CNRS Editions, Paris, 2006
- *Guérir vite - Soigner les angoisses, la dépression, les phobies par les TCC.* Hachette Pratique, Paris, 2005
- *Apprendre à gérer son stress - L'expérience d'un champion, l'expérience d'une vie.* Chiron, Paris, 2005
- *Les psychoses : données actuelles et perspectives.* Elsevier, Paris, 2005
- *Le cannabis : du plaisir au risque - Tout comprendre pour mieux prendre en charge.* Med-Line, Paris, 2005

- *Sur le fil du rasoir - Itinéraire d'un bipolaire.* Ellébore, Collection Champs Ouverts, Paris, 2005
- *Des mots du corps aux maux de l'âme.* Ellébore, Collection Champs Ouverts, Paris, 2005
- *La dynamique de l'équipe soignante en psychiatrie - Les réunions institutionnelles : approches systémique et psychanalytique.* Ellébore, Collection Champs Ouverts, Paris, 2005
- *Dire pour vivre. Pathologies psychiques : témoignages au quotidien.* Ellébore, Collection Champs Ouverts, Paris, 2004
- *Ecarts de conduite. Sécurité routière et psychopathologie.* Ellipses, Collection Vivre et Comprendre, Paris, 2004
- *Cas cliniques en thérapies comportementales et cognitives.* Masson, Collection Pratiques en Psychothérapie, Paris, 2004
- *Observance médicamenteuse et psychiatrie.* Elsevier, Paris, 2004
- *L'information du patient dans le cadre de la recherche en médecine.* Elsevier, Paris, 2004
- *Informer le patient en psychiatrie. Rôle de chaque intervenant : entre légitimité et obligation.* Masson, Collection Médecine et Psychothérapie, Paris, 2003
- *Au-delà des maux. Paroles oubliées ou l'importance de l'écoute.* Ellébore, Collection Champs Ouverts, Paris, 2003
- *L'institution psychiatrique. Le psychiatre, le malade et leur environnement.* Ellébore, Collection Champs Ouverts, Paris, 2003
- *Chambre d'isolement et contentions en psychiatrie.* Masson, Collection Médecine et Psychothérapie, Paris, 2002
- *Isolement, contention et contrainte en psychiatrie.* Rapport de Thérapeutique, LXXXXVIII[ème] session du Congrès de Psychiatrie et de Neurologie de Langue Française, Medias Flashs, Paris, 2000

PREFACE

THE IMPORTANCE OF SLEEP FOR HIGH LEVEL SPORTS PRACTICE, THE IMPORTANCE OF SLEEP IN DAILY LIFE

To practice sports at a very high level, whatever it is, a good quantity and quality of sleep are usefull for athletes. First of all, we have to know that the training of a technique strenghtens while the person sleeps. Indeed, during the night, the mental mechanisms used during the training of the day are reactivated in the brain. During sleep, an uninterrupted exchange of information happens between the different regions of the brain, it allows assimilating information received throughout the day.

If an athlete sleeps insufficiently, training remains incomplete compared with what would have been acquired with a longer sleep.

So therefore, when an athlete learns a new technique or tries to develop new aptitude, it is important that he favours a good quality sleep. If such is not the case, a lot of the accomplished work will be "forgotten", as one might say, by the nervous system, it will not be included, nor "digested". This reason justifies the importance to limit – or even to proscribe – intensive trainings too early in the morning that require a precocious waking going contrary to the needs of the organism.

Not only training is greatly influenced by sleep, but all types of memory withdraw a certain benefit from a rest of good quality.

Don't forget that long-term memory (who allows remembering ancient events) is necessary for the visualisation of a run for example, and during the recall of large concepts as the principles of gravity in relation with movement.

About short-term memory (who allows remembering recent events), we know that it is particularly necessary to record «procedures», who includes the continuity of movements, the identification of our environment and the decision-making.

These two types of memory are improved by sleep, and optimised mainly in the course of some predominating phases at the end of the night. And of course, all these capacities of memorisation are very important for the improvement of athletic performances.

Besides, a good sleep allows a strengthening of the cardiovascular system: the lack of sleep diminishes the speed of adaptation of the organism to an intense effort, for example. During sleep, the majority of your recovery and muscular growth occurs as well. A good sleep also allows balancing the hormonal system. So, in short, sleeping well is necessary for the accomplishment of performances in competition.

And however, even by knowing all of that, several factors lead to the fact that athletes do not train or do not sleep at the best hours. The timing of competitions, the schedules of class or work and parties between friends are so many reasons at the origin of a less optimum use of time by the sportsman at top level. Knowing of the best periods of training according to biorhythms is still not so much spread but it's also playing for something there: the appropriate use of these ideal instants to train or to sleep is a simple element that can improve athletic performances.

Two optimum periods exist for training and performance. There is only one for sleep, which a nap can be added early in the afternoon if needed. Fortunately, these periods make sure that it is easy – biologically at least – to associate times of study and work, training and sleep. So, from 9 PM up to the natural waking, it's the best instant to sleep since the physiological mechanisms of sleep are predominating. A bedtime before 10 pm is therefore desirable for the top level athlete. The optimum length of sleep is very variable from an individual to another one and can also vary for the same person according to different factors. A need from 9 to 10 hours of sleep is very frequent for athletes. About one hour and half is necessary to wake up well and to go against night inertia, which manifests itself by an intellectual and physical functioning still in sub-regime. The length of this period remains unchanged; the type of psychological or driving activation used at this moment doesn't really matter. For some, this period can correspond to the time needed to have lunch and to warm up easily.

A first, optimum period to train comes between about 9 am and 1 pm.

Early in the afternoon, a period of psychomotor slowing down linked to a fall of the level of awakening corresponds to an advantageous period to fulfil some less demanding tasks, and perhaps to make a small nap for those who lack sleep or feel the need to have one after an intense training.

A second optimum period of training follows, between 3 pm and 7 pm.

Then, the body remains in a period of potential performance until 9 pm, but a high level of physical or psychological activation can then harm the sleeping process.

In fact, if sleeping can concerns the athlete of top level or *Mister Everybody*, sleep is an integral part of our existence. However, very few have enough information about the effects of sleep on our daily performances, even if it is about sports, intellectual or more « basic » performances (it is not about a judgement of value there: to care about home, to bring up 3 children, to take responsibility for shopping and for household is not an easier task than the one who consists in running a100 metres, far off!).

Many myths encircle the time when you fall asleep, and deserve that we say a few words about it:

- A first myth says that «*the moment chosen to go to bed is not important*». In fact, the rapidity in which we fall asleep and the quality of sleep is closely linked to bedtime. If two persons sleep about eight hours on night, the one for which the time of sleep is the closest to his natural biorhythm will fall asleep easier and will have a better sleep, thus, allowing a better recovery.

- A second myth is to be known: «*It is possible to train oneself to sleep less*». In fact, there is no technique allowing to diminish the quantity of necessary sleep to the body for the same level of activity. We have no means to control our need of sleep. Some contexts, like stressful or rewarding events for example, can hide our desire to sleep; but this need remains present at the physiological level.

- Here is a third myth: «*Sleeping for a long time during night allows recovering from a lack of sleep*». In fact, several days, even some weeks, are habitually necessary to free ourselves from a debt of sleep. According to the most serious experts in this domain, every missing hour of sleep is recorded and the body will try to get them back. A long night of sleep will perhaps allow filling some recovery, but the body must however keep its rhythm of wakefulness and sleep so the debt of sleep will therefore be able to be "mopped" only after several days.

- Fourth myth: «*It is normal to fall asleep if we are in an annoying situation or when we relax during the day*». Even if it is frequent, it is not normal and it means in fact, a lack of sleep. Drowsiness is a sign of the body that signals us the need to sleep when our night is not refreshing. This need will be mainly felt early in the afternoon, and also when the level of stimulation is low.

- The fifth myth: «*To fall asleep in less than five minutes without waking up at night is a sign of good sleep*». In fact, it is rather the sign of a lack of sleep. In reality, a night of sleep is rather good when we need 10 to 20 minutes to fall asleep, and that there are not much nocturnal awakenings. Besides, sleep is a very good witness of our life during day, because the level of stress or stimulation has a direct impact on our capacities to fall asleep. And when we fall asleep in less than 5 minutes, it means that we need to sleep more. Falling asleep including longer times of awakening can means overtraining for an athlete, for example.

- A sixth and last myth deserves that we still have a word about it: «*Those who sleep less succeed better*». In fact, several studies highlight that the best physical and mental performances are reached when the number of the hours of sleep is heightened. In the same order of ideas, it is wrong to think that sleeping more than the needed hours is a loss of time, and that it can slow us. What is really harmful is to avoid following what the body dictates us by jostling biorhythm by repeated evenings or late mornings sleep during the weekend.

All these general principles, Jérôme Palazzolo gathered them in this work full of practical advices. Living better means that we have to sleep better and those who succeed in life knows how to sleep. A big thank you to Jérôme to allow us to understand better what takes place when we are in the land of dreams.

Christophe Pinna
6 times France Champion of karate
Two victories of the French Cup of karate
Two victories of the Mediterranean Games
6 times European Champion of karate
Two victories in the World Cup of karate
4 times World Champion of karate
World Champion all categories in 2000

FOREWORD

A man who has just made a long journey by car overnight decides to stop to sleep a bit around 6 am before going back on the road a few hours later.

He stops on a parking at the entrance of a big city, at the edge of a wood, to sleep for a moment. But in fact, his parking is a place of passage for joggers of the Sunday morning... And around seven in the morning, he is awakened by a "rat-a-tat" on the window of his car.

The passenger, drawn back of his sleep, opens eyes, winds the window down and asks:

- *Yes? What is going on ?*
- *Excuse me, sir. Could you tell me what time is it, please?* asks the jogger.
- *It is 7:15 !* answers the passenger after a glance on his watch.

The jogger thanks him and went away running.

The passenger goes back to sleep but for short because noises on his window awake him back from sleep again:

- *Sorry Sir, do you know what time is it ?*
- *7:30 !*

The second jogger thanks him and leaves.

Seeing that other sportsmen of Sunday should prevent him from sleeping, the passenger takes a paper, a pencil, and writes the following message: "I do not know what time is it !".

He glues the paper his prominently on his windscreen, then goes back to sleep.

Fifteen minutes later, a knock awake him again on the window:

- *Sir, Sir, it is 7:45 !*

This short story illustrates perfectly different types of insomnia that can spoil your life: that it is disturbances of the time you fall asleep (when you have some trouble to fall sleep), numerous awakenings (you wake up several times in the course of the night then go back to sleep) or of the early waking (you wake up very early without going back to sleep), from the moment where your quality of sleep is bad, the day will be bad as well.

For one French person on four, sleep is a true nightmare: nightmare for those who need hours to fall asleep or to wake up, for those who fall asleep as soon as they sit down somewhere, for those who have to sleep more than 12 hours a day without being in shape... But also for those who lives with them, and who suffer depression or aggressiveness of an insomniac companion, lack of desire and the resounding snores of an apnean spouse or the nocturnal wanderings of a somnambulistic partner.

Insomnia is the most frequent confusion of sleep by far. But how is it possible to define it ? Undoubtedly, as «*a defect of sleep subject complains about*», and it leads straightaway to exclude the "small sleepers" – who only needs 4 or 5 hours without suffering or complaining about it – to include, on the other hand, those, rather many, who complain about trouble and lacking enough time to sleep even if we notice that they sleep in reality about eight hours of, nevertheless, rather good quality.

«Day and night», is one of the most usefull expressions in the French language to describe two antinomic worlds: the first, made of noise and agitation, opposes to the second, made of peace and of serenity. Normally, our organism is programmed to cross from one to another without real difficulty. However, transition is not always simple, and many individuals (more than a quarter of the population) live this phenomenon badly:

  - From some we can say that they know «the day and the day»: for them, the sandman never shows, or in any case, not before early morning. 30% of French say that they are insomniacs and half of them use sleeping drugs regularly

  - Others live in a kind of parallel world defined by «the night and the night». For them, to stay awaken during daytime is a permanent struggle; they fall asleep instantly, everywhere and constantly. 600000 persons suffer from diurnal drowsiness in France

  - The last finally, really see the day and night to succeed one to another, but like a night that looks like a day so much it is agitated. Because they snore, because they suffocate or because they are somnambulistic, they wake up exhausted in spite of their quota of hours of sleep.

Then, many questions settle:

  - Is it possible to learn to sleep well?

  - Are we all equal to sleep?

  - What are the conditions of a good night?

  - Is it possible to recover from the lost hours of sleep?

  - Is it possible to live normally when we only sleep 3 hours per night?

- How to enjoy life when we need 15 hours of sleep daily?
- When the night of someone unsettles the night of another one, how to go out from the hellish spiral?
- What is the impact of sleep on the awaken life?

In short, can a low quality of sleep be at the origin of a real disability?

I will try, in this work, to enlighten you on different existing forms of insomnia that can poison your existence. Simple methods, more coming from good sense than from psychology, psychiatry or pharmacology will allow you to live this physiological phenomenon better, one that worries so many persons.

Finally, I hope to persuade you, with these few chapters, that the land of dreams is not so frightening as it seems to be...

I. TO UNDERSTAND SLEEP AND INSOMNIA

The contemporary research on sleep started in the middle of the XIXth century, but thanks to the contribution of modern technology, it's possible to understand better what happens when we sleep today. However, you have to know that in the XXIth century, we are still not able to go farther than simple theories to explain factors that launch and support sleep.

Scientists are far from having clarified all the mysteries of sleep when we fall asleep. As for *Mister Everybody*, we would really like to know why we spent a bad night again...

Experiments made on animals highlighted the primordial role of sleep in the regulation of the temperature of the body, the maintaining of an optimum health and why we get good physical and intellectual performances. The deprivation of sleep unsettles the internal balance of the body, endangers health and can, eventually, lead to death. Other studies have to be made so that we could understand perfectly why we sleep.

A regular sleep is also necessary for human being as to eat or to drink. A new-born baby sleeps 16 to 18 hours a day during the first weeks of his life, a five-year-old child 11 - 12 hours. Between his 15th and his 50th year, men needs from 7 to 9 hours of sleep on average. With age, the need of sleep diminishes (5 - 7 hours are enough in general).

1. Tiredness:

When quality and/or quantity of sleep are not good, the body begins to show a few signs of tiredness. Generally, these signs are known to the person and to her circle (for example, I know that if my wife doesn't sleep enough, she is going to be in a bad mood all day long). It is important to never neglect these warnings sent by our body because they are alert signals that encourage us to have a rest:

Main signals of intense tiredness
- Heavy eyelids, «burning eyes»
- Blured sight, eventually hallucinations («mirages»)
- Drowsiness
- Though articulation, slow speech, heavy elocution
- Confused ideas, broken thought
- Endless yawns
- Difficulties to hold the head straight up
- Difficulties to communicate
- Headaches, stomacaches
- Difficulties to care about little but probably important details
- Bad mood, loss of motivation (sensation of being «out»)
- Impairment of cognitive capacities (memory, focus, perception)
- Enhanced distractibility and irritability
- Doubts concerning the way to take initiatives and decisions
- Reaction time becomes longer
- Increase of mistakes and reduction of tolerance to mistakes
- Loss of the sens of humor
- Tendancy to exagerate problems

- Tendancy to take useless risks

- Increase of time of response, decrease of reflex.

Whatever our efforts can be, we will never succeed in eliminating completely our need to sleep. We cannot either diminish our time of sleep with impunity. Quickly, tiredness makes us vulnerable in some ailments and predisposes us to errors and accidents. Quality and quantity of sleep have direct influence on our level of alertness and performances. In fact, it would be possible to define tiredness as «a progressive fall of physical and psychical alertness that can lead to sleep».

- **Physical tiredness** generally appears after an intense activity or a very long working period (have you never pointed out that we are always exhausted in the course of the week preceding holiday?). Then, cramps, muscular stiffnesses and various pains come to remind us that it is time to have a rest. A state of weakness and a fall of endurance are habitual in that case.

- **psychical tiredness** is as for it, linked to an uninterrupted psychological tension (for example: the fear of the salesperson of non accomplished sales fixed by his manager), in a heavy load of intellectual work (for example: the annual accountancy accomplished just before the tax return), or even in excessive worries (for example: the anxiety of the student that has his exams). At first, psychical tiredness makes more and more difficult to remain concentrated on a definite task. Memory is less and less efficient, which leads to a quick loss of information. The capacity to make adapted decisions begins to decline and the person has more and more trouble to fit to new situations. He is therefore going to make more and more efforts to avoid making a mistake, thus it will increase its psychical tiredness. As you can see, a vicious circle is formed:

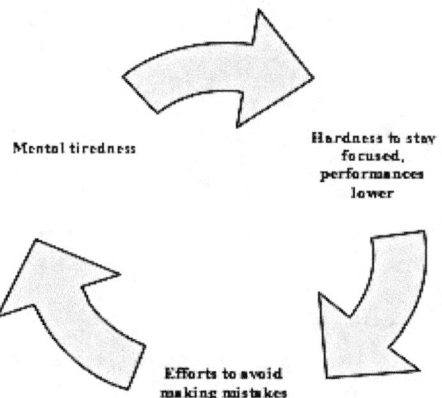

Mental tiredness

Hardness to stay focused, performances lower

Efforts to avoid making mistakes

If the lack of sleep continues, episodes of "micro-sleep" can happen. In the course of these phenomena, the person dozes off literally during a few seconds. This type of event is not rare. We were all victims of micro-sleep by watching TV, by reading or by fulfilling other tasks routine. Generally, after such episode, we wake up suddenly without being able to remember what has just been told or taken place (besides, I have some memories of such situations in the course of my schooling…): we feel like having been victim of a kind of "absence". And of course, the more we are tired and the more the frequency of micro-sleeps augments.

When we drive, the phenomenon can considerably increase the risk of accident. A driver taken by a micro-sleep of barely 4 seconds and who drives at 100 kilometers an hour, for example, moves on a distance of about 110 metres during his drowsiness, it's the length of a football field! This kind of absent-mindedness can have very serious consequences.

From this perspective, a team of New Zealand[1] researchers worked on the number of road accidents caused by tiredness (and not about alcohol, nor medical substances nor a mechanical problem) in the course of day: even if results concern principally New Zealand, they bring to light the tendencies that can be noticed worldwide. So, the number of road accidents caused by tiredness augments appreciably in the middle of the night, following midday and evening meals (the famous "slump" that follows good lunches and hearty dinners):

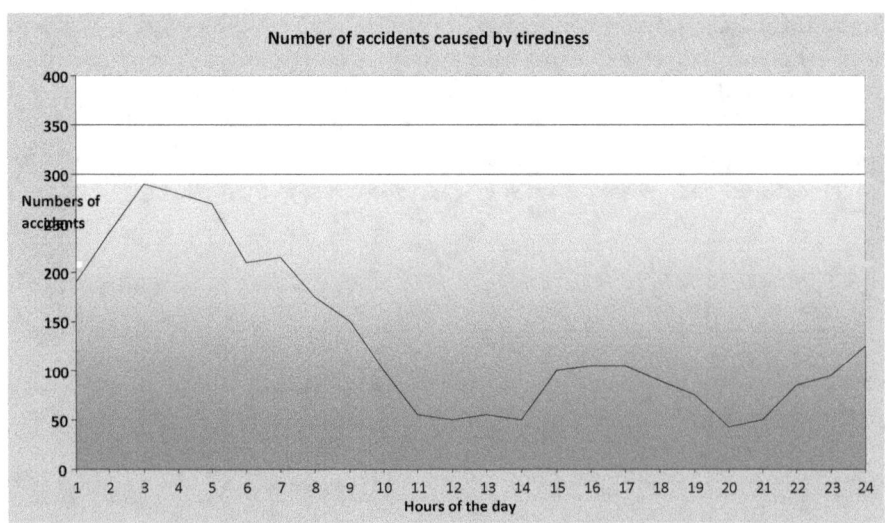

---

[1] Gander PH, Marshall NS, Harris RB, Reid P: *Sleep, sleepiness and motor vehicle accidents: a national survey.* Aust N Z J Public Health 2005; 29(1): 16-21

In the professional world, it is the same thing: several scientists worked on accidents that happened within different firms (heavy industry, nuclear power stations, petrochemical plants, road transport). All results converge: the night corresponds to the period in the course of which most errors and accidents happen, just followed by the middle of the afternoon and the beginning of the evening (after lunch and dinner).

Besides, many of notorious disasters occurred at an instant when the technicians were in duty for a long time, they were working at night or hadn't slept enough…

2. Sleep:

Modern research allowed us to define what we call "the architecture" of sleep. In fact, the depth and the characteristics of this one vary in a foreseeable way in the course of night. A young adult in good health falls asleep generally 10 - 20 minutes after having lain down and put the light out. His night is composed of 5 different stages of sleep that happens alternately and in a cyclic way:

So, from the moment we fall asleep, your thoughts begin wandering and your conscience of the external world diminishes (this period corresponds to the stage 1).

The stage 2 represents 50 - 60 % of night; it is a stage of relatively light sleep (I mean that it is rather easy to wake up in the course of this stage).

Stages 3 and 4 are defined as being a phase of deep sleep because in the course of this period, a much more intense stimulation is needed to awaken the sleeper. These stages happen mainly in the course of the first night half. Put together, stages 1 to 4 represent **the slow sleep**.

Paradoxical sleep (also called the REM sleep, from the English *Rapid Eye Movement* which means quick movements of the eyes) appears about every 90 minutes in the course of the night. It is so possible to expect 4 - 5 episodes of paradoxical sleep by night. The first episode is generally very short, during less than 10 minutes, while the last one can last more than one hour. The majority of the paradoxical sleep occurs therefore in the second half of the night. Actually and recently, we thought that paradoxical sleep was the elective period of dreams. In fact, it is possible to dream throughout the night, but it is well in the course of paradoxical sleep that our most notable and the strangest dreams occur[2]. The bar chart below shows how an adult in good health crosses the different stages of sleep in the course of a typical night:

---

[2] We must be aware that sleeping pills shorten dream's lenght at the end of the night.

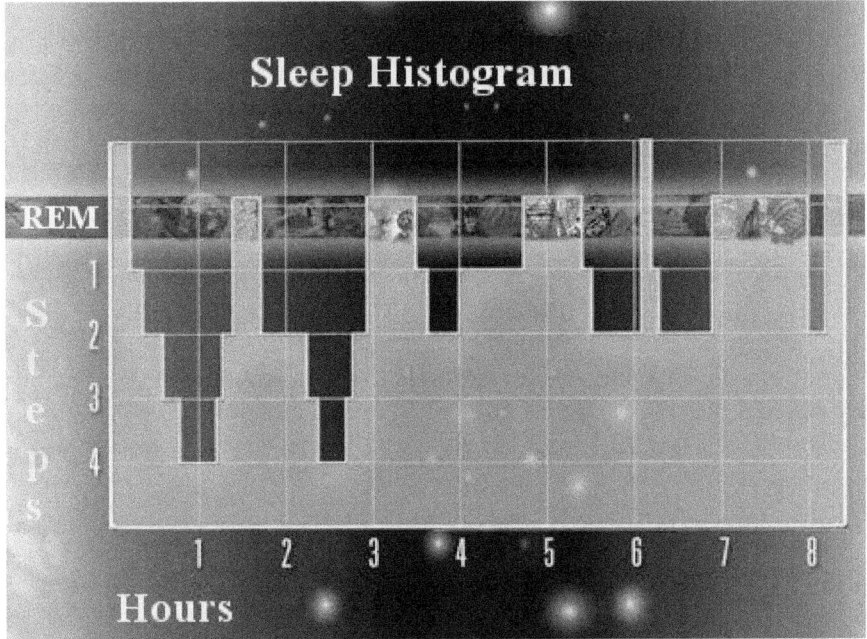

- 4 stages of slow sleep: 1 = the lightest sleep, 4 = the deepest sleep
- 1 stage of REM sleep = *Rapid Eye Movement* = paradoxical sleep = main period of dreams
- At the beginning of the night, we STAY more in a period of deep sleep
- At the end of night, the period of dreams is longer

3. The length of sleep:

Many patients I see in consultation ask me following question: «*How many hours of sleep do I need, doctor?*». In fact, the minimal length of sleep necessary for our good functioning has been determined by various scientific studies. All results converge: the man needs uninterrupted sleep of at least 4,5 - 5,5 hours in each 24 hours period. It is really a minimal length, meaning that if habitually you need your 8 hours of sleep to attend to your daily occupations, this time of 5 hours will allow you «to work correctly» during a few days. But you will not be able to hold two or three months in a row with this rhythm ...

Besides, if you do not give to your body the quantity of sleep it needs to recover, and this, during barely three or four days, you must know that your level of alertness will be also bad as if you exceeded levels of alcohol in blood allowed by law. Therefore, be careful if you must drive your car or mechanical devices after some sleepless nights...

Several experimental works proved that short periods of rest (short naps from 10 till 20 minutes) taken in regular intervals in the course of day could partly fulfill the need of sleep, and assure a minimal level of performance. But a warning must however be made: the attained levels of performance when normal sleep is replaced with a sequential sleep (short naps) are always lower compared to ones of the attained levels of performance when we are perfectly rest !

4. The study of sleep:

From all times, we prescribed a rest on bed for sick people, without really knowing exactly what was going on when the person was sleeping (everybody remembers the famous "sleep therapies" recommended in depression during the last century). In our times, even more disturbed, charged with various tensions and numerous stresses, a growing number of women and men cannot get a really refreshing sleep anymore. This situation is even more annoying as we cross near a third of our lifes in the lands of dream (a 60-year-old man will therefore have slept 20 years!). So, scientists elaborated a way to study what takes place when someone sleeps: it is the polysomnography.

The polysomnography is an examination associating the sleep recording of a person with the recording of several other physiological activities as breathing, muscular contractions at the level of legs, movements of eyes, cardiac beating, etc.

To highlight the different stages of sleep, electrodes are put at the level of the scalp (it allows to record the electrical activity of the brain), around eyes (it allows to record the movements of eyes) and at the level of the chin (it allows to record muscular activity):

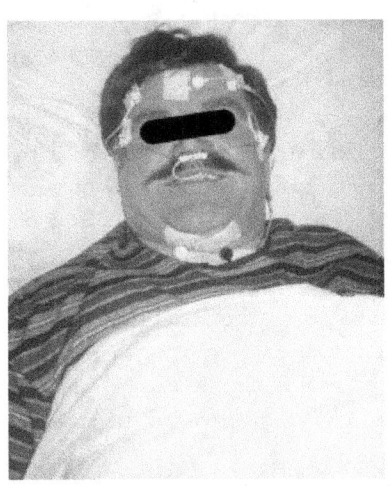 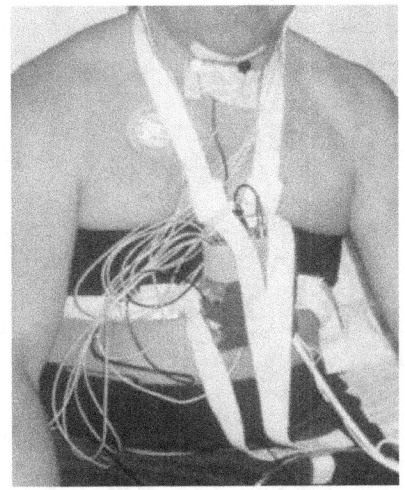

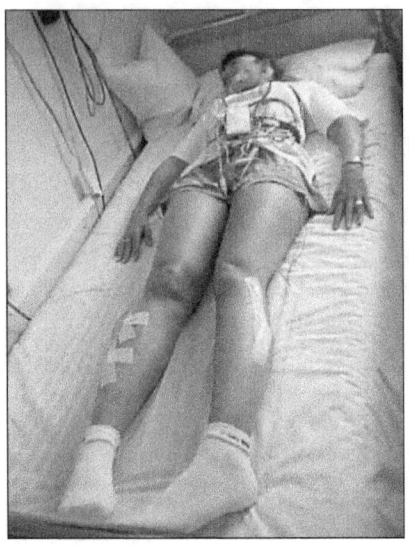
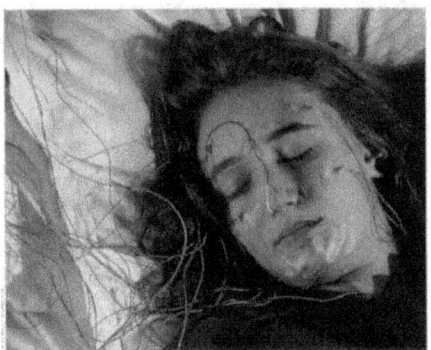

The polysomnographic records showed by the pictures are used to study different problems or diseases that can be at the origin of a sleep trouble.

A normal night of sleep includes 4 - 5 cycles, every cycle last about 1:30 - 2 hours and is constituted by two stages (a stage of slow sleep and a stage of paradoxical sleep). Let us see more in details together, of what our nights are made:

● Everything begins with **slow sleep**. About thirty minutes after the the person fells asleep, the electroencephalogram highlights waves with a lower frequency than with those found in a state of wakefulness, but with a higher amplitude. In other words, these waves are less and less frequent but larger. During this stage, muscles loosen, the temperature of the body falls, breathing and cardiac beating decelerate, and arterial pressure diminishes. This "fall of speed" can besides be at the origin of "small anomalies": a muscle loosens faster than another one, causing a sudden twitch or the fall of blood pressure in the internal ear (where the sense of balance is located) is transmitted in the brain like an impression of sudden fall and the sleeper wakes up suddenly.

This stage of slow sleep, of a complete length about 90 minutes, is constituted itself as we saw, of four stages of increasing depth:

- During stage 1, eyes are closed and the person begins to relax, he can progressively feel floating. The electroencephalogram shows waves called *alpha* and *beta* waves. These waves are progressively replaced with even slower waves, called *thêta*. Contact with the external world decreases, but the awakening is immediate if the sleeper is stimulated.

- In the course of stage 2, the electroencephalogram becomes irregular; the amplitude of waves recorded at this instant is high. These waves get organised in characteristic faces. The waking begins to become more difficult and, interesting to be noted; one bad sleeper on two asserts not being asleep when he is awakened during this stage.

- In the course of the stage 3, sleep becomes deeper and deeper and a new serie of waves appears: these are *delta* waves. Vital signs (temperature, blood pressure, heartbeats, breathing) begin to decelerate, and muscles are relaxed. At this stage, which intervenes about twenty minutes after the beginning of the stage 1, dreams are frequent. It's generally at this instant that many sleepers start to snore. Because of the muscular slackening, the soft palate vibrates under the influence of the movement of the air, causing an unpleasant loud noise to be heard for the spouse who tries to have a rest...

- In the course of the stage 4, the electroencephalogram shows many *delta* waves [this is for this reason that we speak of slow sleep: this stage is characterised by a change in the electrical activity of the brain (slowing down of the electrical waves and increase of their amplitude)]. At this instant, vital signs attain their lowest level; while the alimentary canal works at full speed (it is the reason for which we say that a nap favours digestion). The muscles of the body are relaxed but the sleeper changes of position every 20 minutes on average. If he is stimulated, he will really have a lot of trouble to wake up from his sleep. Besides, it is during this period that enuresis occurs (the person urinates in the bed) and somnambulism (the person gets up and does something while he still sleeps).

• **Paradoxical sleep** happens about 90 minutes after the person fell asleep. Waves found on the electroencephalogram change roughly and become very irregular. *Alpha* Waves – even if they are characteristics of the stage 1 – appear. The temperature of the body augments, the heart starts to beat faster, breathing accelerates, blood pressure rises[3]. The activity of the alimentary canal, as for it, diminishes. The brain uses a large quantity of oxygen, undoubtedly much more than when the individual does not sleep.

The recorded waves resemble those of the waking state; this is what gave the name of *paradoxical sleep* to this stage. Paradoxical sleep was also called REM sleep (from the English *Rapid Eye Movement*), because eyes move fast

---

[3] It explains the happening of heart attack or cerebrovascular accidents vasculaires during the night for certain « high-risk » persons.

under eyelids during this period.

If the sleeper is a man in good health, an erection occurs while he dreams. Similarly, an increased blood irrigation at the level of the clitoris is noted for women. In the same way, the body of the sleeper is literally "paralysed" during the stages of paradoxical sleep: a complete muscular slackening occurs. This paralysis allows the body to avoid making the movements the person makes in her dream. It also explains this feeling we have in some nightmares: we would like to go away but we feel as stock-still. For some researchers, the movements of eyes could be in direct relation with the dream itself. Finally, we know that we remember our dreams much better if the waking takes place during paradoxical sleep.

Every cycle of sleep is accompanied by the secretion of different hormones in blood: for example, the body secret large quantities of growth hormone at the beginning of the night. This one is essential for the regeneration of our cellular tissues. But you can feel relieved if you do not find sleep: your hormonal system also begins to work since you are simply lying down and in state of drowsiness!

The first stage of paradoxical sleep of the night lasts only a few minutes. Then, a new cycle of about 90 minutes with a stage of slow sleep happens. During this second cycle, the stage of paradoxical sleep is a little longer in general than the first one. These cycles of 90 minutes succeed one another during all night. From the second cycle, the stage of deep slow sleep (stages 3 and 4) begins to shorten to disappear completely in the morning with the last cycles of sleep. On the other hand, the stages of light slow and paradoxical sleep (stages 1 and 2) become longer as the night advances, and the chance that the sleeper wakes up augments. To wake up in the course of the night is besides inseparable of a healthy sleep: after long stages of deep and paradoxical slow sleep, the body has to be able to turn over to assure a good circulation of blood. And yet, this change of position can be made only if the brain stays alert during some instants. Generally, these stages of awakening are so short that the sleeper even doesn't memorise them. It is only from the age of thirty years that most individuals are aware to have woken up during night.

Let us sum up on the picture according to what takes place while we sleep:

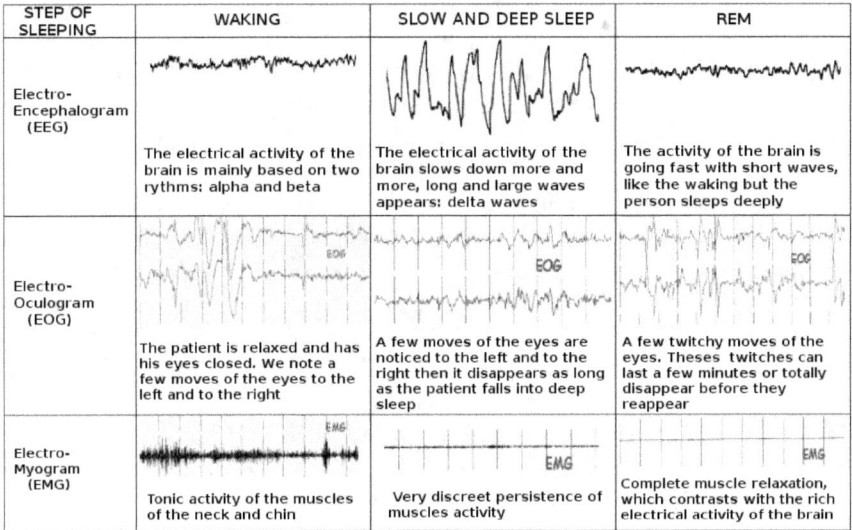

STEP OF SLEEPING	WAKING	SLOW AND DEEP SLEEP	REM
Electro-Encephalogram (EEG)	The electrical activity of the brain is mainly based on two rythms: alpha and beta	The electrical activity of the brain slows down more and more, long and large waves appears: delta waves	The activity of the brain is going fast with short waves, like the waking but the person sleeps deeply
Electro-Oculogram (EOG)	The patient is relaxed and has his eyes closed. We note a few moves of the eyes to the left and to the right	A few moves of the eyes are noticed to the left and to the right then it disappears as long as the patient falls into deep sleep	A few twitchy moves of the eyes. Theses twitches can last a few minutes or totally disappear before they reappear
Electro-Myogram (EMG)	Tonic activity of the muscles of the neck and chin	Very discreet persistence of muscles activity	Complete muscle relaxation, which contrasts with the rich electrical activity of the brain

Then, after this explanation, are you still persuaded that sleep is a passive phenomenon ?...

5. Dreams:

Dreams take a very important place in our life: every night, we spend about one hour and a half to dream. From all times, men tried to understand the signification of this phenomenon. Psychology allowed us to raise a part of the veil, by linking up dreams with the unconscious, but it is necessary to know that today even dreams are far from having delivered all their secrets...

As we saw, dreams can happen any time when we sleep. For a long time, we thought that they occurred only during paradoxical sleep, but now we know that all stages are concerned. However, intensity and sens of reality of dreams differ according to the period during which they appear: for example, even if they can happen at the beginning of drowsiness and during short naps, they are more itemised and contain more activity during paradoxical sleep, particularly in the last night period.

Many people complain not to dream. In fact, it would be fairer to say that they do not remember their dreams: the research in laboratory showed that practically we all make the experience of dreams during our sleep.

The origin of dreams remains, since Freud, the object of many debates. Dreams are mainly constructed from our daily experiments. Traditionally, we incorporate in our dreams, under a form or other one, events that occurred during the day. It was however shown that for the older persons, dreams could concern situations dating of 50 or 60 years before![4]

Age, sex, sociocultural levels... of a person have an influence on its dreams. For example, a child is going more often to imagine animals than human beings; men will going to be more often victims of anxiety and physical attacks than women.

Dreams are therefore in narrow relation with our awaken life. Two points are however worth being underlined in this respect:

> - Firstly, the experiments of awaken life represented in dreams are generally very distorted, it means that in most cases, only the sleeper can understand the meanings
> - Secondly, the large majority of dreams are not enjoyable for the sleeper: we have tendency to live events of our daily life in a negative way in our sleep (even those who were positive at first)

Even the most painful dreams (these bloody nightmares that disturb our nights and that still worry us in the waking) must not be considered to be harmful elements: in fact, they mean that something inside of us tries to solve a conflict, a difficulty, a suffering. Our dreams search compromises tirelessly between reality and our own perception of things: even if they are

---

[4] Barad M, Altshuler KZ, Goldfarb A: *A survey of dreams in aged persons*. Arch Gen Psychiatry 1961; 4: 419-424

frightening, they manifest the extraordinary vitality of our unconscious, they are the intimate voice of it.

Some traumatisms can be at the origin of intense and regular nightmares. So, it is not rare that in a state of post traumatic stress (after a natural disaster, an accident, an assassination attempt, a war) the person live again such horrible situations in dreams. In that case, the help of a psychotherapist can be considered.

By raising to the surface overnight, what affects us "in the background" during day, dreams allow us to unload our internal tensions and prevent us a large number of disturbances (aggressiveness, stress, anxiety, somatizations). Besides, they play an important role in our capacities of memorisation.

Moreover, it is good to know that some artists drew inspiration from their dreams to write or to paint famous pieces nowadays: the representation of reality distorted by dreams can lead to pictures and very creative associations! For my part, I know several scientists who made important discoveries after having tested them in dreams.

«*Make of your life a dream, and of your dream a reality*», said Saint-Exupéry.

II. TO UNDERSTAND WHAT KIND
OF INSOMNIAC YOU ARE

1. Be wary of erroneous information:

First of all, Insomnia defines itself according to indications given by the person with a sleep disorder. Several types can be noted:
- Disturbances to fall asleep and of sleep maintaining
- The premature waking
- A spontaneous sleep neither long enough, nor enough refreshing

As soon as we are based on the assertion of somebody who sleeps badly to define insomnia, it is obvious that it is not easy to make ourself a precise idea of what this trouble is. When someone is going to consult his doctor for this type of disturbance, the affection is generally installed for a long time, and the person has already tried all "tricks" that the neighbour, her grandmother or the baker gave him. And with the development of the Internet, "biased" advice won't miss. You can judge by yourself:

● *«The full beneficial effects of the yellow topaz:*
Drop of yellow light, the topaz treats jaundice by analogy and all diseases linked up with the liver; it is efficient against the virus of influenza, mental diseases, visual disturbances, hemorrhoids, varixes and hemorrhages. This stone is also advantageous in cases of asthma, gout, insomnia; it would treat on the epilepsy. The topaz favours love affairs; it preserves emotional troubles and cool down storms. Spiritually, it is symbol of action, affection, benevolence, joy, freedom, knowledge, sympathy and calmness. It is the emblem of friendship and of affability, happiness, constancy and contemplation». So, Anita, one of my patients was 43-year-old when she went to see me for the first time. She suffers from insomnia for 8 years, and guess what? she bought this stone on an Internet site for the modest sum of 450 euro! Her sleep did not

improve but her wallet got lighter in a notable way...

- *«Protector of the habitat:*
The protector of the habitat is a very efficient and aesthetic geological "radiowaves effect" equilibrium maker to harmonise your habitat. It's aimed to resolve problems of telluric origin that harm the places we live in. It was conceived to be put in your house (home, office, flat) as an icon! and it became "the first radiowaves icon".
The protector of the habitat has special feature to act on physical (damaging waves of telluric origin) and spiritual plans (damaging waves linked to spell and negative entities (larvas and ghosts). The protector of the habitat is unique and of a formidable effectiveness. For houses of large surface and for an optimal result, we recommend the instalaltion of four balancing devices put down at the four cardinal points: north, south, east, and west. Here are some results obtained with the installation of four protectors of the habitat:
> *- Better sleep (insomnia disappears),*
> *- Alleviation of anxiety,*
> *- Better resistance to diseases,*
> *- Children study better and are calmer».* Of course, you will be able to recuperate a good quality of sleep only if you invest 240 euro here...

- «Message from the professor M:
"There are thousands of people who call me to consult regarding their love affairs, their health or their business.If there is a problem I resolve it directly, adding that improvement will be noted in the following week.
Then why do you stay with your suffering and your difficulties?
There is always a good solution that can satisfy you for the rest of your life".
The professor M is the descendant of a sage who had a good reputation with the governors' commanders-in-chief at the time of colonies: it's him who was named big Marabou of Western Africa for the first time. It's here that everything has begun; then his wisdom was known in Africa, more precisely in Guinea on the set of Fouta-Djalon.
Today, there are millions of people who come to see him. Since he practices his art, insomnia and suicide disappeared in all countries "centered" by the professor M». On this Internet site, you are promised – in exchange of money – to remove your sleep troubles by a simple mail (however written by the professor M himself).

Examples are numerous. Anyhow, without arriving at such ends, a lot of people are ready to try "everything" as soon as they have the promise that they will find a good quality of sleep. It clearly demonstrates the lack of comfort given by insomnia! However, it is necessary to know that this affection can be treated completely in an adapted way, as far as we know where the problem is, and how to approach it.

The adresse of the insomniac person allows at first to see if he has not realistic waitings concerning his sleep, in length and continuity. In this respect, I remember Nora, a young 27-year-old patient who wished that I prescribe her a medicament that would make her sleep 15 hours a day, because she was mainly searching to stultify herself in a way to forget an unhappy love affair!

When we met an insomniac person for the first time, it is important to know if his habitual behaviour during the night (what is called the *hygiene of sleep*) is likely to prevent a regular and refreshing sleep. In this respect, I will name the example of Petro that goes to sleep at 3 am on Mondays, 2 am on Tuesdays, 4 am on Wednesdays. He goes out in nightclub a lot, drinks some alcohol regularly in the course of his parties. It is not amazing that he feels some difficulties in falling asleep at 10 pm on Thursdays…

If the hygiene of sleep is good and that the expectations of the person are realistic, it is necessary to know if insomnia results from a known illness that can be specifically treated, or if it is about as we say, a *primary* insomnia, that is to say without obvious medical reason.

Finally, it is important to have an idea of the repercussions of the confusion of sleep (does the person arrives at the point that he is not able to work anymore, for example?) and of its intensity (does the person fall asleep one hour after he went to sleep or if he spends sleepless nights)?

2. To define the trouble even better:

Insomnia is one of the most often heard complaints by the general practitioners. We have to know that 15 % of Europeans people complain of quality or quantity of their sleep, and that one Frenchman of five says that he has trouble to sleep. Other facts are important to know:
  - 85 % of sleep troubles are never diagnosed (even not recalled by the patient during a visit to his doctor)
  - 20 - 30 % of traffic accidents on motorway are due to tiredness and to people who fall asleep when they drive
  - 14 % of Frenchmen take drugs to sleep – what is called hypnotic, sleeping drugs – (10 % of men and 17 % of women), against 6 % of Europeans.

When the person speaks about it to her general practitioner, in 15 % cases it is about a chronic insomnia, dating from more than 6 months. And of course, before going to their doctor, various tricks, more or less adapted, have been tried: this *self-medication* goes from the simple preparation to exaggerate old remedies (milk and honey, hot-water bottle) or medicines of plant origin, and even techniques of relaxation (relaxation therapy, yoga), of available sedative drugs (sometimes more toxic than those prescribed on prescription), or even some alcohol or other toxins (cannabis for example). The time spent in the bed is generally extended, in a hope of finding sleep.

Very often, the answer given to somebody who suffers from insomnia is an almost automatic prescript of hypnotic; in this respect, an American study[5] showed that among 536 patients who had accepted sleeping drugs, only 12 % were questioned concerning the origin of their trouble of sleep. It means that for 88 % interviewed persons, a sedative drug was prescribed without going farther than the simple questioning: «*Do you sleep well now?*». It is therefore important, before going to see your doctor to ask him «*a little something to help you to fall asleep*», that you understand well the mechanisms of sleep, and that you could apply some simple techniques I will develop farther.

---

[5] Shorr R, Bauwens S: *Diagnosis and treatment of outpatient insomnia by psychiatric and non-psychiatric physicians.* Am J Med 1992; 93: 78-82

3. Then, insomnia?

Oh well, by insomnia, we have to understand a reduction of quality and of length of sleep, or even a bad recovery.

- The medium length of sleep of the European who slept well is currently of 7 hours but can vary from 5 to 10 hours on night
- It is often the length of time we need to fall asleep that poses problem at first. Generally, there is around 30 minutes between the instant when we lie down and the instant when we fall asleep

Some authors propose to calculate the efficiency of sleep: we just have to make the link between subjective length – that is to say the number of hours that the person thinks to have slept – and the complete time spent in the bed. Normally, this report is superior to 85 %[6].

The insomniacs complain about a bad quality of their sleep which draws some uneasiness in the course of the day (tiredness, angryness, and difficulties in concentrating, blue mood). In this respect, if you think to have problems of drowsiness, it can be interesting to consult the Appendix 1 (ladder of Epworth).

- **Clear definition:**

The DSM IV (Diagnostic and Statistical Manual of Mental Disorders, fourth edition) defines primary insomnia[7] precisely: it is characterised by a complaint concerning the moment the person fall asleep or the maintaining of sleep, or even the presence of a not refreshing sleep, during at least a month. This problem is at the origin of a marked suffering of impairment of social or professional functioning, or in other important domains. The disturbance of sleep is not linked to a physical illness, to a psychical illness or to a substance (medicine, toxin).

The persons who introduce a primary insomnia often complain about difficulties to fall asleep in relation with intermittent awakenings during sleep. Less often, these persons can complain only about a not refreshing sleep, it means that they have the feeling that this one is agitated, light or of bad quality. Primary insomnia is often linked to an increase of alertness overnight, a phenomenon which goes together with an anxiety linked in a search of sleep. A suffering and a marked preoccupation linked to inability to fall asleep can contribute to the development of a vicious circle: the more

---

[6] Example : Yesterday at night, I went to bed at 11 :30 PM; this morning, I woke up at 7 :30 AM and I went up directly (then, it means that I spent 8 hours in my bed); I think that I've slept around 7 hours in all. So, the ratio is: 7/8 = 87,5%. Oh! The efficiency of my sleep is correct!

[7] At the opposite of insomnia which has a defined origin: physical illness (breathing trouble), psychological illness (dépression, stress), and use of drugs…

the individual tries hard to sleep, the more he is frustrated and worried, and the less he is able of falling asleep. To lie down in a bed in which we had many white nights may be at the origin of frustration and of conditioned awakening (saying: « *I am not going to close the eyes overnight*» yet cost to be conditioned to never be able to sleep). Conversely, the person can doze off more easily if he does not try to reach it hopelessly (for example, it is not rare that an insomniac falls asleep regularly in front of television, by reading or by driving his car). Some individuals bring back that they sleep better elsewhere than in their own bedroom, far from their habitual conditions.

To summarize:

Diagnostic Criteria of a primary insomnia according to the DSM IV
A. The predominant complaint is a difficulty to fall asleep or staying asleep, or a non-restorative sleep, for at least one month. B. The sleep disturbance (or associated with fatigue during the day) is the source of a significant distress or impairment in social, occupational or other important areas. C. The sleep disturbance does not occur exclusively during a physical, mental, or substance use.

• Important points:

This definition of primary insomnia has the merit to specify several points:

1) It gives a criterion of length: we speak about insomnia only after one month of evolution (or more). Then, please, do not rush on a hypnotic after an unpleasant night!!! Such behaviour will have as the only consequence to make you dependent in the small pink pill that will make you sleep. And afterwards? You will have to take the small green pill to awake you in the morning, the small white pill to avoid you to stress during the day, and the small blue pill to have a satisfactory erection? We have the right not to be competitive one day, to spend a difficult night, without having to stuff ourselves with drugs![8]

2) The confusion of sleep gives rise to an important suffering, or can have a not negligible impact on the life of the person (at social, professional levels, or in other domains). So therefore, somebody who sleeps not much but who lives well is not insomniac; on the contrary, an individual who does not succeed any more in doing his work correctly as he

---

[8] And don't forget that it's the words of a psychotherapist!

is too much tired because of his bad quality of nights must be helped.

3) The person who does not succeed in sleeping because he has backache does not suffer from primary insomnia. It is about a secondary insomnia there (cf. farther).

This few details are important because the treatment will differ according to situations. From simple information – let us take the case of Roger, he went to see me on August 18th because he finds it difficult to fall asleep for 2 days; he fears heat (in summer it is very warm in Nice): he is out of question to prescribe him a hypnotic for a long duration – in specialised prescription – Jean, who does not sleep because he suffers from dreadful pain at the level of the back, will receive a prescription for a sedative analgesic rather than a hypnotic – every therapeutic answer is unique and must be adapted according to an individual way.

4. The origin of insomnia:

Insomnia can have different origins. If you do not sleep well, if your sleep is not refreshing or that you wake up too early, it is important to search a reason in your problem of sleep. And in your reasoning, it will be necessary to determine, with the help of your doctor, if you suffer from a primary insomnia or a secondary one, relative to another affection. In the latter case of the problem, your insomnia can be:
- The symptom of a health problem happening at night (for example a respiratory difficulty during sleep)
- linked to a psychical illness (for example a depression or an anxiety)
- linked to a physical illness, to a consumption of various toxins (for example the absorption of alcohol before going to bed, the presence of an angina pectoris or an asthma).

Let us sum this up on the following diagramme[9]:

---

[9] According to Entenmann W, Schwander J, Strub M: *Insomnie chronique : symptôme ou diagnostic ?* Forum Med Suisse 2003; 42: 1000-1007

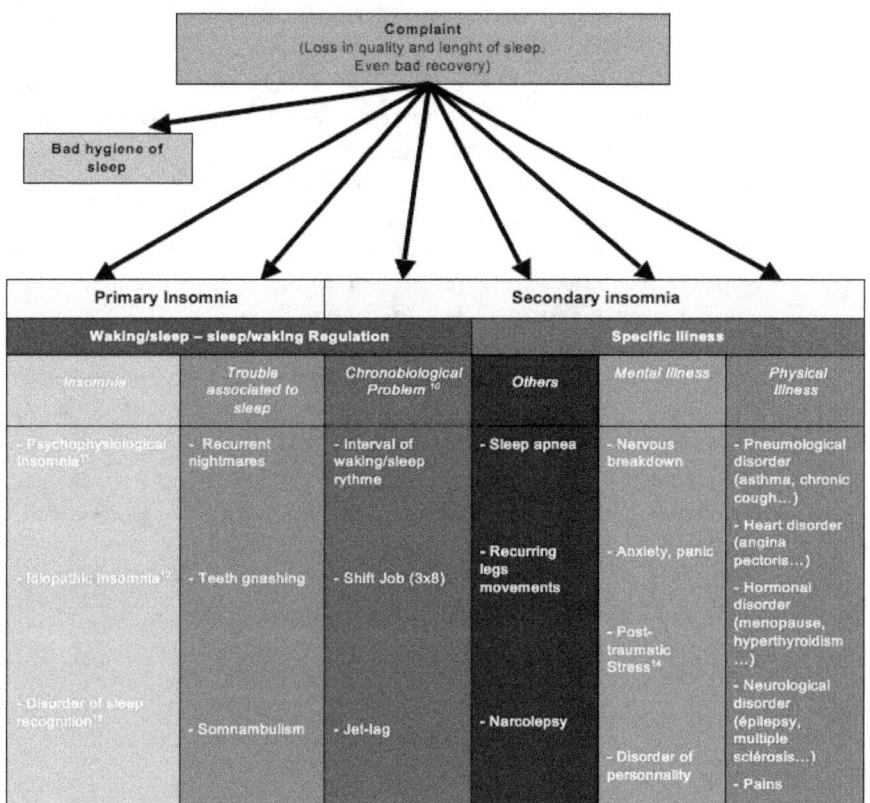

Complaint (Loss in quality and lenght of sleep. Even bad recovery)					

Bad hygiene of sleep

Primary Insomnia			Secondary insomnia		
Waking/sleep – sleep/waking Regulation			**Specific Iliness**		
Insomnia	*Trouble associated to sleep*	*Chronobiological Problem [10]*	*Others*	*Mental Illness*	*Physical Illness*
- Psychophysiological insomnia[11]	- Recurrent nightmares	- Interval of waking/sleep rythme	- Sleep apnea	- Nervous breakdown	- Pneumological disorder (asthma, chronic cough...)
					- Heart disorder (angina pectoris...)
- Idiopathic insomnia[12]	- Teeth gnashing	- Shift Job (3x8)	- Recurring legs movements	- Anxiety, panic	- Hormonal disorder (menopause, hyperthyroidism ...)
				- Post-traumatic Stress[14]	- Neurological disorder (épilepsy, multiple sclérosis...)
- Disorder of sleep recognition[13]	- Somnambulism	- Jet-lag	- Narcolepsy	- Disorder of personnality	- Pains

---

[10] Chronobiology is the science of biological rythmes living beings are subject of.

[11] It's a conditioned insomnia, acquired, depending both from psychological factors (fear of falling asleep, anticipatory anxiety of searching sleep without falling asleep), and physiological factors (the subject «preconditions himself» to avoid to sleep, generally, without being conscious of).

[12] Namely, for which we haven't find an apparent cause. One of my master was saying that about this subject: *«The term ''idiopathic'' means that the doctor stays ''idiot'' (ignorant) and that the patient stays ''pathic'' (suffering)».*

[13] The person forgot that he slept whereas he has a good quality of sleep.

[14] Post-traumatic stress is a kind of anxiety following an extreme traumatizing specific event on the psychological level (terrorist attack, war, serious accident, act of God, physical violence, rape...).

As soon as your doctor will have determined the origin of your sleep disorder, it will be easier to implement a strategy to allow you to spend good nights again.

But anyhow, the majority of the discussions I had with my insomniac patients highlight the fact that the problem of sleep is intimately linked to a situation of stress. The individual emotional reaction (anxiety, irritation) and the appearance of a maladjusted behaviour in relation to the moment they fall asleep play an important role in the installation of insomnia.

Main factors of maintaining insomnia are:

- Important worries concerning insomnia and its consequences in relation to the performances and the well being of the following day («*Phew... It is three o'clock and I still do not sleep... Tomorrow, I will be completely exhausted for my presentation!*»)

- The presence of negative predictions («*Ouch... As I have just woken up, I won't be able to go back to sleep for the rest of the night*»)

- The installation of inefficient strategies to find sleep that, in fact, are only augmenting the feeling of frustration of the person who extends his time in bed for nothing

- Maladjusted use of hypnotics or even alcohol consumption or consumption of toxins (cannabis for example)

5. Think about the psychical disorder:

It is not rare that one of my general practitioners colleagues says to me: «*Yesterday again, I saw a patient who complained about sleeping disorder. He found it difficult to fall asleep, he woke up early in the morning and was feeling tired throughout the day. Finally, he was in a full nervous breakdown without being aware of it*». Even if insomnia can have, as I have just explained, many reasons, there is one that we don't right away suspect – either because we don't think about it, or because we refuse to think about it: the psychical illness.

Psychological affections are often accompanied by sleep disorders, but these last are generally considered as commonplace. In certain cases, they sum up the complaint made to the doctor. Disguised psychological request for aid or negation of the psychical dimension of insomnia, the approach of the person is sometimes ambiguous and doesn't ease the task of his practitioner. Most often, it is about a secondary disorder of sleep to a diffuse anxiety or to a starting depression but it can also be about a more serious illness. To spot the subjacent psychical affection is still complicated due to the fact that any bad sleep can have psychological consequences to the individual.

• The point of view of the psychoanalyst:

The relation between a sleep disorder and a psychological affection is complex. We therefore have to isolate, of the person who complains about difficulties to sleep, the specific role played by each of these two elements. The doctor will also have to take care about the global functioning of the sleeper: he is going to have to keep in mind that the perceptible discomfort has to be taken into account to offer the most adapted treatment. But he will also have to be attentive to the psychical state of his patient, in fear that his request, in relation to sleep, hides no more serious psychological affection. Sleep disorders are frequent in psychiatric practice: they are quasi constant with the hospitalised persons' and touch more than half of the subjects seen in consultation.

• Insomnia and disturbances of mood:

Sleep troubles and mood disorders are often linked: present in more than 25 % of cases of insomnia, depression is one of the too often misread main reasons. Moreover, insomnia is one of the most often found symptoms in the course of depression (actual in 80 - 95 % cases according to studies). It is indeed exceptional that in consultation, a depressed patient does not complain about the bad quality of his sleep. Sometimes even, this complaint occupies literally the front of the scene, even so to conceal other symptoms and then, to be at the origin of diagnostic and therapeutic errors[15].

Focus : To recognize depression
Depression can manifest itself brutally but, generally, it is caracterized by the progressive development in a few days by (not to say in a few weeks) :
- An unexplained sadness with remorse associated to a feeling of disuse and despair
- A cognitive slow down
- A big tiredness
- A loss of interest, not to say a disguss for life
- An insomnia,
- A refusal to eat with a loss of weight
With time, a lack of self confidence with feelings of depreciation and guiltiness appears and suicidal ideas that might be expressed or covered. A delirium can be noted in this case.

For the depressed person, the moment when he falls asleep is not really disturbed. Even in certain cases, it can be moved forward and quicker than usual. On the other hand, the sleep is broken by numerous nocturnal awakenings, and especially shortened by a precocious awakening, leaving the subject tired, exhausted, with mind frozen in the black perspective of a new day. The frequent association of a significant anxiety to depression aggravates the division of sleep by many awakenings and leads to an increase of the delay the person fall asleep.

In 10 - 15 % of cases, depression manifests itself only by an excessive drowsiness in the course of the day. This particular form is more frequent for the teenager or the old person.

---

[15] I remember about the case of Laura, 42 years old, who received a lot of hypnotic drugs from her doctor during 2 years in a row even though she was presenting every symptoms of true depression. Her only moan during these 24 months has been: «*Doctor, I can't fall asleep. Your sleeping pills are not strong enough!* ».

At the the opposite, in case of maniacal bout[16], insomnia is the norm. Manifesting itself by difficulties to fall asleep and numerous awakenings during the night, it sometimes precedes fit, and then, it constitutes a well known early warning sign, feared by the circle of the sick person. The considerable shortening of the time of sleep is generally made without any feeling of tiredness – at least at the beginning – and is accompanied by a state of euphoria and excitement.

Focus : How to identify the maniacal bout

• Most often, the maniacal bout happens suddenly. Sometimes, an emotional shock, a disease, taking drugs or toxiques substances can help to cause its appearance. Insomnia and excitement are strong at the beginning. The person surprises his circle by his restlessness, his sudden joviality, or even his ill-considered spendings.

• In a few days, troubles increase :

- Self confidence is exagerated

- Hyperactivity is obvious, with gesticulation, insomnia, attempt to fulfill many tasks without achievement

- Mood is effusive. The attitude that looks like joviality at start turns quickly to familiarity or even rudeness. The ill person becomes seductive, really histrionic

- A quickened thought, associated with frequent change of subjects, make all kind of linear discussion impossible

- Insomnia is practically always present without being associated to the feeling of tiredness (this is important and dangerous: the person literally become exhausted without being aware of it!).

Sometimes, bouts are less marked and physical and cognitive hyperactivity only remains with sleeping disorder: then, we talk about hypomaniacal access.

---

[16] Please note that the term *maniac* doesn't describe a tidy and ritualised person: in psychiatry, such a person should better be defined like being *obsessional*. We meet the maniacal fit in the *Bipolar Disorder*, formerly called *manic-dépressive behaviour (PMD in French)*.

• Insomnia and psychosis[17]:

Psychosis is often accompanied by very important sleep disorders in most cases. Insomnia is one of the first symptoms to appear, and can precede the constitution of the typical psychotic picture by some days. Generally, the length of sleep is reduced; this reduction can be due to a strong anxiety, to difficulties to fall asleep and numerous awakenings in the course of the night. Sometimes, the delirium itself can prevent the person from having rest (for example if he always hears voices that speak to him, round the clock).

The polysomnography shows that the sleep of the person suffering from psychosis is very broken up. The study of awakening during the night does not reveal particular predominance at some point. In certain cases, a complete inversion of the wakefulness-sleep rhythm can be observed (the person sleeps in daytime and is awakened at night). The excessive drowsiness during daytime is rare, generally due to the prescript of sedative medicaments.

From the 1970s, a reduction of deep slow sleep for the schizophrenics, particularly during the stage 4 was highlighted.

It is important to note that antipsychotic medicines improve sleep quickly, often long before correcting delirium.

• Insomnia and anxious disturbances:

▪ Insomnia and confusion panics:

The panic confusion, defined by the happening of repetitive, unforeseen, severe panic attacks, without triggering visible cause, made the object of many research works. The polysomnography shows among the persons who introduce a panic confusion, some difficulty to fall asleep associated to a less effectiveness of sleep and a significant increase of the body's movements in the course of the stage 2. These persons do not have anomaly of the paradoxical sleep. Sometimes, nocturnal crises of panic are noted during the transition of the stage 2 to the stage 3.

▪ Insomnia and generalised anxious confusion:

Our life is full of issues and challenges that often create worries and anxiety. Anxiety is a normal emotion; a moderate anxiety can besides be invigorating to perform some tasks. But when anxiety is excessive, it becomes pathological and manifests itself by physical and psychical

---

[17] To be short, a psychosis is a psychological illness leading to break with reality: the person see things, ear or perceive things that exist only in his mind (this is what we call a *delirium*). Schizophrenia is a psychosis.

symptoms; worries are then permanent and abnormally exaggerated: it is what is called a generalized anxious confusion.

The sleep of a person who suffers from this type of confusion is unsettled in general. We note a difficulty of falling asleep and to maintain a correct sleep in polysomnography, and a reduction of the length of deep slow sleep (stages 3 and 4). A reduction of the length of paradoxical sleep is also rather characteristic.

Actually, the sleep of anxious subjects singles out by a difficulty to fall asleep, a difficulty to maintain sleep linked to a weak effectiveness and an instability translated by frequent changes of stages. Moreover, there is a large changeability from a night to the other one.

● **Insomnia and post traumatic stress:**
The state of post traumatic stress[18] is accompanied in most cases by many impairments of sleep: reduction of the complete length of sleep and of its effectiveness, difficulty in attaining paradoxical sleep and reduction of deep slow sleep (stages 3 and 4) has been highlighted by the polysomnography.

Studies were accomplished to get a better differentiation of nightmares linked to the post traumatic stress from other types of dreams. They underline that the traumatic dreams take place generally earlier in the cycle of sleep, between one and three o'clock, out of paradoxical sleep, and that they are often linked to movements of the body while the "usual" dreams of anxiety happen in the two or three last hours of sleep.

● **Insomnia and insanity:**
The old person faces normal modifications of his sleep, especially with the appearance of a sleep broken up by numerous nocturnal awakenings; then it is frequent to determine the presence of a nap in the course of the day.

When insanity[19] takes place, periods of agitation and disturbances of behaviour can happen, more particularly in the course of the evening, or even during night time. Little by little, the awakening/sleep rhythm is reversed, giving rise to the classical picture of the turbulent and mentally ill

---

[18] It's a set of reactions that can develop inside a person after he/she lived, has been the witness or has been confronted to a major traumatism. Generally, it's an event that caused the death of other persons or serious injuries, or implicated a threat of death or major injuries and caused an intense terror, a feeling of helplessness or horror. Such an event can be an accident, a violent aggression, a rapt, a hold-up, a hostage-taking, a fire, an earth quake, a flooding...

[19] Like Alzheimer desease, for instance.

person, agitated during the night, but drowsy and apathetic in daytime. Sedative medicines and hypnotic prescripted hardly improve this picture, and have a rather negative effect resulting in disturbances of memory and confusion but they are sometimes necessary to relieve circle and family.

6. When insomnia rhymes with noise:

The noise, which is on the way to becoming one of the nuisances the most important of the city, can be at the origin of an important problem of sleep. When we sleep, we are not completely cut of from the external world, and we continue to react to the stimulations of our environment. Our hearing works as well during our sleep as in broad daylight. And even if we do not receive the precise signification of a noise while we are in the Land of Dreams, every perceptible sound is treated by a very specific zone of our brain.

The effects of noise on our night of rest can be measured in a subjective way (that is to say that the person expresses his perception and his feelings), or in an objective way (that is to say thanks to the polysomnography).

● **The subjective effects** of noise on sleep are studied by giving questionnaires to the sleeper as soon as he will be awake. Questions concern the perceptible quality of the past night, as well as the discomfort given by noise. These subjective effects are important to study, because it's the essential of the complaint we have in consultation (you cannot imagine the annoyances of living next to an airport or to a railway station can be created for the patients I see regularly...). Of course, results obtained by this type of inquiries have to be put into perspective, because sometimes the complaint concerning noise during the night means, in fact, a global annoyance to the person in relation to its living conditions in general... Besides, answers given by the sleeper can be influenced by different factors, which have nothing to do with the real level of noise: the kind of house (flat, single-family home...), the social situation of the person (active, retired, in unemployment, in Minimum Benefit), relations with neighbourhood, etc.

● **The objective effects** of noise on sleep are much more difficult to assess. The polysomnography remains generally the prerogative of the laboratories of sleep. However, studies made in this domain show that noise can be at the origin of several types of annoyances:

- It delays the moment you fall asleep (we all have the souvenir of a night where we do not succeed in finding sleep because of an uninterrupted and irritating noise: we turn, we move, we are irritated and finally we can't find rest because we focalize on the disruptive noise![20]);

- The numerous awakenings during the night[21], knowing that irritation can still prevent from going back to sleep fast (in the center of Nice, it is frequent to be awakened in summer by party-goers going out from nightclub, and after howled them to be silent, it is difficult to find sleep again)
- The morning waking caused by noise (for example, by the garbage truck that comes to pick up garbage cans, or by the neighbour who puts the radio on at 7 am, when he gets up[22]).

The polysomnography also highlights some effects of noise on organism:

- There are modifications of the electrical activity of the brain, with a more or less important impairment of the structure of sleep according to intensity and repetition of the disruptive sound. Then, it is possible to find a sensitive reduction of time passed in some stages (notably slow sleep, or even the paradoxical sleep)
- An acceleration of breathing and of beating of the heart, often linked to an increase of blood pressure, is noted
- Body movements are more and more frequent and intense, going of the simple displacement of an arm to the total change of position.

These reactions can be observed on an isolated way, or linked each others, again according to the intensity and repetition of the noise.

On long run, the effects of noise are hard to study because they can happen in more or less long term, and they are not very specific.

On the contrary, it is possible to easily appreciate the state of tiredness and the mood of a person the day after a night disturbed by noise[23]. This valuation is in general the only criterion remembered by the doctor to appreciate the impact of a sound disturbance on the sleeper. In fact, it is the perception of discomfort that conditions the protests of the individual and that determines its behaviour, sometimes encouraging him to take a sleeping drug.

The use of thorough tests, generally maded in a laboratory, allows assessing

---

[20] I personally lived this situation recently when my friend Philippe went to sleep at home. This brave Philippe is used to go to sleep lately, watched television until 3 in the morning! And, if it wasn't enough, he snored until 6... We hear him in the whole appartment.

[21] For instance like when Philippe cough and sneeze (he even had a cold!).

[22] Or by Philippe when he has to go back home by the first plane and slam the door when he leaves.
My advice is to never invit Philippe to sleep at home!

[23] Mark my words, do not upset my wife the day after a bad night!

the impact of noise on sleep and on intellectual performances. Besides, samples maded in urines and blood reveal disturbances suffered by organism.

Let us sum all this up on the following picture:

Impacts of a sleep disturbed by noise on the long run
- Extreme chronic tiredness - Drowsiness during daytime - Drop of vigilance (increased risks of accidents) - Fall of performances - Fall of motivation at work - Anxiety - Palpitations - High blood pressure - Increased risks of heart attack - Increase of adrenaline and noradrenaline blood level during night[24] - Increase of cortisol blood level during night[25] - Drop of immune system - Mental health disturbances[26]

---

[24] They are the hormones of stress; the raise of these levels have consequences on heart and blood circulation.

[25] It's a hormone linked to the degree of agression of the organism, it plays an essential role in the immunitary system.

[26] Noise is considered to be the main disturbance for people suffering from anxiety disorder or a nervous breakdown. Presence of this factor plays a decisive role in the evolution and the worsening risk of these illnesses.

Without being alarmist, it is allways better to favour a calm environment during sleep, don't you agree?

● Noise and environment:

Noises are not equal, and they don't have the same impact on our sleep. Moreover, for a given noise, effects are variable because they can depend on other linked factors, and some of them are directly linked to the sleeper exposed to sound aggresion, to conditions in which this attack takes place…

It is also necessary to know that noise can be uninterrupted or intermittent, stable or fluctuating: these characteristics are important to take into account, because they will directly have an influence on the quality of sleep of a person: a fluctuating or intermittent sound is very disturbing in general because he stimulates our attention (and it's, you have to admit, upsetting enough when we try to fall asleep).

Next to the physical characteristics of a noise, you should not forget the importance of his signification. Indeed, a noise with a particular signification has a very important «awakening power» (for example: a baby who cries in the middle of the night will awaken his parents more easily than the zoom of a motorbike that passes on the street, even if the intensity measured is the same in both cases).

● Noise and profile of the sleeper:

As for the very sleeper, age plays a not negligible role in the noise/sleep relation: if the child – contrary to common belief – is also sensitive to noise as the adult, problem differs for the old person. This last is particularly vulnerable to every cause that could come to disturb its sleep, and this phenomenon is accentuated by a generally long and difficult nod off.

The impact of noise on sleep is also linked to the sex, but age still has an influence at this level: from 18 to 30 years old, men are more sensitive than women to sound attacks while they sleep, while this tendency is reversed in the course of ageing.

The psychological profile of a person also has an influence on its own sensitivity to noise: so, the presence of a rather obsessional personality will draw away a very weak tolerance for everything that concerns a loud environment.

Focus : Obsessional personality

The obsessional personality is a kind of personnality caracterised by these points :

- The person suffers from a constant problem with order and cleanliness

- The person is very meticulous

- The person is always very ponctual

- The person is perfectionist

- The person is very scrupulous with is work

- The person is trusty, respect for his commitment and duties

- The person finds it difficult to share

- The person knows how to save money, sometimes to greediness

- The person has a personal taste for owning, he tends to possess much things (he is often a collector)

- The person is obstinated, has a sense of perseverance, tenacity and others can't easily change is mind

- The person is unfriendly at first

- The person tends to place everything on an intellectual plan

- The person can hardly let the things go on freely on a love affair

- The person is rarely touched by distress or existential crisis

Some kind of professions creates a particular sensitivity to noise during sleep. It is for example the case of night-shifts schedules because the person is then subjected to very high sound levels when he dozes off, in the course of the day.

The effects of noise on organism also depend on the stage of sleep in which the sleeper is. So, impact diminishes as they pass of a stage of light sleep to a stage of deep sleep. It is however necessary to know that awakening becomes easier and easier as the combined sleep time augments.

Of course, the use of sleeping drugs influences the reactivity of the sleeper to noise, this fact could create a problem if, for him, there is a need to intervene fast in the course of the night (in case of fire or about a domestic accident of a child, for example). We will go back to this fact later, but it is important to underline here that the use of hypnotic must remain **punctual** and **exceptional.**

7. My child finds it difficult to sleep...

In fact, it is really possible to see sleep troubles appearing from young childhood. To the very preschooler, temporary or not very intense disturbances are especially noticed, but sometimes real insomnia can be found. Between 5 and 12 years old, the continuity of sleep is going to improve, but this one can be flustered by what is called parasomnies, such as nocturnal terrors, nightmares, somnambulism, talking while sleeping, rythmes changes of sleep, bruxism or enuresis.

● The temporary sleep troubles:

Generally, a confusion of sleep for the child is due to a temporary and particular circumstance. In most cases, when this one sleeps badly or does not succeed in falling asleep, it is because his own needs and rhythm imposed by his parents are not in adequacy. To this, let us add the anxiety of his father and of his mother in front of such trouble of insomnia – with sometimes some dramatisation of the confusion – and then we are locked in a hellish spiral that grows in the course of time.

Habitually, some discussions with the family allow to understand better its functioning, its habits, and to identify the problem at the origin of insomnia. Then, we ask the parents to fill an agenda of sleep for their child; it makes the diagnosis easier.

In general, sleep recovers easily, by respecting some very simple advices.

The sleep confusion in question can be owed to the way of life established by the parents (maladjusted timetables[27], bad habits[28]...), on environmental conditions (light, high volume of television), or a too copious meal taken in the evening or even in the absence of borders (generally when the child, towards the age of 2-3 years, asserts its authority[29]).

---

[27] It is unbelievable to know that children of less than 10 years old are going to sleep at 11:30 PM or midnight, after the movie and even the last TV forecasts when they go to school the day after...

[28] Like sharing your bed with your child.

[29] A few parents sometimes talk about real tyrany!

● True insomnia:

When the child introduces a true insomnia, it is then necessary to search a physical or psychological origin, such as:

- *A gastro-œsophageal low tide*, it's very frequent for the new-born baby, and is translated by chest pain and regurgitations that interrupt sleep
- *An allergy or a particular intolerance to a food* that can draw away a difficult sleep
- *Apnea of sleep*[30]
- *ENT troubles*, such as otitis
- *Social and/or psychological problems within the family* (frequent disputes of the couple, mother or father themselves in psychical disturbances…)
- *The anxiety of bedtime*, linked to a separation, to the fear of the dark…

● Parasomnies:

• *The nocturnal terrors:*

Screams, terrified look, fast heartbeats, speeding up breath, sweats… the nocturnal terror is a real crisis of panic! Happening with children habitually between three and six years, this type of problem happens at the beginning of the night (within the three hours following bedtime). The child is then at the last stage (stage 4) of slow sleep: he sleeps deeply and is going to enter in a stage of paradoxical sleep. In the case of nocturnal terrors, this transition, for an unknown reason, occurs badly, causing a state of intense and loud agitation. The child does not wake up, and even if he opens his eyes, he sleeps however outright; he won't remember anything the following morning! Neither monsters, nor ghosts, nor wolves are to accuse, as during a bad nightmare (happening rather at the end of the night, it awakens oftenly the child and cause difficulties to fall back asleep)!

• *Nightmares:*

Nightmares happen generally during paradoxical sleep. They are very frequent for children. Fear can be very intense, but contrary to the nocturnal terrors there are few physical demonstrations. In general, pictures and history are perfectly spotted by the child. If its age allows it, he will

---

[30] It has the characteristic of a stop of breathing for a duration of more or equal of 10 secondes, the resume of breathing occurring at the same time with a very short wake up. These apneas can have cardio-respiratories, neuro psychiatristic, social and scholar consequences. It is therefore important to detect it shortly.

even be able to explain it in detail. Even the babies who begin barely speaking, try to explain to their daddy and their mom what they lived in a dream.

An intense nightmare often leads the child to want to sleep with his parents, to refuse to go back to its bed because he is afraid to go back to sleep, with a fear to go back to bed alone and to find what scared him in its nightmare. But be careful, because if the situation is repeated, it risks becoming a bad habit. The parents who allow to their son or daughter in the grip of the bad dreams to sleep with them give them the following message in reality: «*If you wake up at night, instead of trying to go back to sleep alone, come to join us*». This former incident opens the door to a fast understood behaviour, which will be long and difficult to transform!

• *Somnambulism:*

Somnambulism is a frequent affection; we think that 15 % of children make at least one crisis of somnambulism in the course of their life. It is more frequent for boys; it appears towards the age of 4 years old and, in general, disappears in the puberty. In many cases, the presence of the family medical history is found.

Typically, the access of somnambulism happens one to three hours after the subjet has fallen asleep, and can be repeated two to three times in the same night. The child gets up, has the eyes largely opened but he seems to see nothing. The face is inexpressive. He wanders slowly, his step is often clumsy (he bashes everywhere).

During the access of somnambulism, the child can sometimes fulfil rather elaborated tasks: he can eat, take some drink, etc.

He is perfectly tame and he will easily be convinced to return in his bed; even if it means that he will get up again a bit later. Episode lasts in general some minutes to half an hour.

Somnambulism does not represent particular danger. In rare cases, it can involve what is called "risky" somnambulism, with escalation of a cupboard, of a balcony, or even an unexpected exit outside home. Simple safety regulations (as locking doors and windows) are enough in general to limit the risk. Sometimes, it is necessary to use sedative medicaments, at least for a short-term period.

In fact, this type of access is due to an "incomplete waking" of the brain, which happens habitually during the deep slow sleep. It is the reason why the child doesn't remembers what happenned the following morning.

It's useless to awaken the somnambulistic child. It is better to bring him back calmly to his bed. And as he remembers nothing, it is not recommended to talk again with him about his waking the following day. It would be a useless risk of worry for him. We also have to know that even if he gets up overnight, the child will not be especially tired the following day.

• *Sleep Talking*:

The somniloquia means that the the person talk during sleep. The Sleep Talking episodes can happen during slow sleep and/or in paradoxical sleep. The episodes that happen during the paradoxical sleep tend to be more elaborated. In fact, it represents a somnambulistic equivalent to be minimised.

• *The rythmies of sleep*:

It can be made of movements of the head from back to front or lateral movements from the right to the left, or even movements of swing of the torso or of the body, backward and forward, when the child is on his knees or on all fours. This rythmies starts towards the age of 6 to 9 months, and always before 18 months. They are generally made by boys (in 70 to 80 % of the cases). This rythmies have a variable intensity but when movements are violent, they can hurt the head and create bumps...

They start before the child fells asleep and continue during the light slow sleep. Their emergence is sometimes favoured by psychological factors. Habitually, the rythmies of sleep disappears spontaneously around the age of four. Their persistence for the normal child will lead to the practice of a psychological balance sheet. No treatment is habitually necessary, but it is sometimes recommended however to take measures to avoid shocks (padding of the bed, mattress on the soil). For the older child and in case of intense crisis, it is necessary to search for problems of emotional order, and to struggle against anxiety. It is rare that we are led to prescribe a tranquillizer or an antidepressant.

• *The bruxism*:

The bruxism is the act of grinding one's teeth during sleep. Banal demonstration for the child, it can lead, in extreme cases, to the use of a gutter during the night to avoid that teeth get damaged by rubbing some them on others.

• *Enuresis*:

Enuresis – or wee in the bed – defines itself as «*the happening of a complete and unconscious micturition, in the course of the night but also during the nap, for a child of more than 3 years old that introduces no urinary infection or neither organic anomaly, nor any neurological or psychiatric affection*».

Many studies show that 15 % to 20 % of children from 5 to 6 years old are concerned, and twice more frequently for the boys than for the girls. At the age of 10 years old, there are more than 6 % of kids who still wet their bed, and 2 % of the 15-year-old teenagers are still in close touch with this problem. These figures do not take into account young adults who do not dare to speak any more about their disability but who however have to live with.

Although the hereditary character of this trouble is often recalled, enuresis is not an illness in the strict sense of term, but rather a problem of development. The person concerned introduces simply a weakness of the vesical sphincter. The vesical sphincter is the muscle that closes the bladder. As soon as the urine collected in the bladder attains some volume, the sphincter, too weak to keep it, loosens and causes an involuntary emission of urine.

Then, to sum up, what kind of attitude should I take during the night awakenings of my child?

The problems of bedtime :

- Many children cry at bedtime because they need to be secured. If this is the case with your son or your daughter, be patient. Just tell him/her calmly but firmly that it is time to sleep, the day is over. Once your child is calmed down, get out of his room (do not induce a maladjusted ritual where you will have to stay with him to help him to find his sleep).

- The moment to go to bed may be experienced as a painful separation for your child. He can then begin to cry, ask you to come see him several times, complaining about a thousand pains. In such cases, return him to bed every time you come back to his room. Then, it is likely that he starts to make a whim, to whine, to cry ... Do not scold him, stay with him, but do not hesitate to be firm: tell your child that you are tired and that you are also going to bed. He needs to understand clearly that it is time to sleep, and that you are decided to enforce this rule. Remember that your child will be more "tyrannical" when he feels indecision in one of his parents. You can also give him/her a hug, calm him down by singing a lullaby. Thus, he will be able to integrate the following diagram: BED – sEcuritY – REST. Explain him/her that he has to sleep alone in his room, that there is nothing to fear, and you are close to him in the next room... If this is not enough, you can install a night light and / or leave the door slightly open.

Nocturnal fears, nightmares :

- In case of nocturnal fears, it's better to avoid talking to your child, or to light up. Lie him down again quietly. It is useless to try to reassure him, he is in deep sleep. If these fears are too frequent, we can consider a timely treatment, or to reinstate a nap in the afternoon if needed. Anyhow, consult your doctor before giving any medication to your son or daughter.

- In case of nightmares, the best is to calm your child, to talk to him, to comfort him, and make him tell his bad dream... If he rushed into the parents room, scared, very anxious, you must reassure him, cuddle him, and then escort him in his room, talking to him.

Don't do that :

- Do not think that if you put your child to bed later, he will sleep better. Instead, he will miss sleep because usually he will wake up at the same hour the next morning.
- At night, avoid games where the child becomes agitated and angry (like fighting or "tickle!").

- If a nap is important for young children, it should not be too long or too late in the afternoon, because it may then disrupt his sleep overnight.

- If no specific disease has been diagnosed by your doctor, you should know that giving your child a hypnotic is useless, and can even be dangerous to his health.

- Do not awake completely a child involved in a night terror or sleepwalking, it would only add to his confusion and it could risk giving him an unnecessary anxiety.

- Do not give your child a bad habit of falling asleep in your arms or in your bed. Inevitably, he will awaken in the night and will then realize that he is alone in his room. And so, at that time, he'll start to cry...

- Do not present sleep as a punishment. When you scold your child because it is too turbulent, you may already have come to let you say: "*If you continue to heckle, you'll go to bed!*"? Would it be possible that subconsciously we push our children to think that going to bed corresponds to a kind of punishment rather than to associate the rest to a privileged moment? In such a case, if the punishment is repetitive, you should not have to be surprised of the resistance of your little darlings to go to bed...

To do, when you have a baby :

- Establish a bedtime ritual: for example, give him a bath, read him a story, then let him drink a last bottle, all of this will take place at the same time and always in the same order. Try not to shift this ritual over an hour on weekends, a time when the hours are always more flexible.

- Try the technique of the kiss: Lie down your baby, leave it for a while and go back to kiss him before he has time to cry. Your baby will feel less anxious in the long run to be left alone and he will fall asleep naturally because he will have understood that you always return to kiss him.

- If your baby is crying around ten minutes, let him alone: it is a way for him to get his sleep. And when he wakes up, do not get him right away, so we should leave him alone a few moments. Be aware that, from birth, if the baby cries and her mother immediately took him in his arms, he will integrate the fact that crying will provide him the arms of his mother immediately.

- Leave the door open so your baby will hear the sounds of the house, the radio on, the sounds of pots and pans. This reassures him more than it disturbs [31].

- You need to help baby to find his marks in time so that its sleep cycle settles in the best possible conditions. We'll have to score at birth the contrast between day and night. We must therefore make him sleep at night, in darkness. You will have to stop the activities that are likely to wake him, knowing that during the first month, a quiet sleep is very superficial.

- During the phase of troubled sleep, you won't have to worry, and not to wake him up. When baby is awake, he is calm, he looks around him. He expresses himself if he is hungry, have no doubt about it!
- Don't let your baby fall asleep in your arms before depositing him in his bed. You have to let him sleep alone very early.

- Give your baby a small blanket or clothing impregnated with your scent. Reassured, he can associate it with the ritual of falling asleep.

---

[31] Knowing that everything is relative: if you listen to hard rock songs very loudly, you'd better have to isolate your baby!

- Turn your alarm clock against the wall: it's amazing to see that we feel better in the morning when we don't know that we woke up at one, two, three and five o'clock in the morning…

- The sleep hours of the baby must be respected. If he sleeps, the fact of by passing his bottle or the feeding of the night is not a problem. At the opposite, don't hesitate to give him to eat if he wakes up because he is hungry.

- Sleep when your baby has a nap during daytime. Obviously, it's a bit complicated to do when we have one or more children to care of but even half an hour of sleep can be really more than relaxing at the end.

- You will have to respect his naps during the day avoiding to move around, making too much noise that can annoy, tire or irritate him. In such cases, your baby won't sleep enough and cry frequently.

- Don't forget these words: your baby is like a « parabolic reflector»: he «captures» and feel the stress of his parents. Thus, a "cool" mamy and daddy will get more chance to have a calm baby, especially during the night.

III. SIMPLE ADVICES TO SPEND A GOOD NIGHT

● At first: some simple rules to be respected

At first, it is important to know that physical activity favours sleep. But to help you to spend a good night, this activity must be regular (an occasional intense effort has rather tendency to disturb sleep in the course of the following night) and never practiced just before bedtime (nocturnal jogging before going to bed is not recommended). Regular, daily exercises, contribute to a balanced rhythm of wakefulness/sleep[32].

As we talk about before, many persons have tendency to take a hypnotic as soon as they spend a bad night. However, solutions that are preferably based on common sense than on psychological and/or medicinal intervention exist.

Here are some advices to follow before rushing on a sleeping drug:

Adjust your environment
1. Sleep in a safe, comfortable and restfull place.
2. Choose you bedding carefully – you spend a third of your life in it! –. A bed too comfortable or not can be the source of back pain. Keep your bedding in good condition (frame, mattress).
3. Cut yourself against external aggression (noise and light). Your bedroom should be quiet and dark. If the noise bothers you, use a pair of hearing

---

[32] No need of a marathon everyday: the simple fact of practicing a good walk can be sufficient.

protection plugs. If the light bothers you, install blackout drapes on the windows or wear a mask over your eyes.

4. Ventilate and humidify your room before going to bed. If necessary, place a damp towel on the radiator (to be avoided if you have a heater!), or install a humidifier.

5. Find a suitable temperature for your bedroom (between 18 to 20 °C), and make sure it remains constant during the night.

6. Hide your clock if it displays time. Being aware of the rest you have lost and seeing the hours scrolling are particularly stressful.

Good to know :

Five major synchronizers can help us to respect a satisfying sleep-wake rhythm:

- Day / night alternation (light / dark),
- Time you wake up (that must be regular and not too late)
- Hours of meals
- Physical exercise
- Social and professional constraints

If any of these synchronizers no longer fulfills its function (eg. the person has no exercise during the day, if he remains mostly lying or even, the socio-professional constraints are constantly changing, such as in some random times jobs), sleep will inevitably be disrupted.

Maintain a healthy sleep

---

1. Respect regular hours when you go to sleep or wake up.

2. Avoid important "shifts" during the weekend (night awaking, sleeping late).

3. Be vigilant concerning the nap after lunch: you must know that we are programmed to sleep a certain number of hours per day. If your body is programmed to sleep eight hours and that your nap lasts 2 hours, it will be as much time as you will not spend sleeping at night. If you are tempted by a nap, sleep every afternoon or not at all, but in any case, less than 20 minutes!

4. Have regular physical activity in the morning or early afternoon, but avoid any strenuous exercise before bedtime.

5. Do not drink beverages containing caffeine or theine after 16 hours.

6. Avoid alcohol after dinner. A "small glass" to fall asleep disturbs sleep more than it helps, and can cause early morning awakening.

7. Try to relax before going to bed: a bath but not too hot, music, reading a simple book... Try to pamper yourself a little bit!

8. Avoid heavy meals and foods difficult to digest before going to bed.

9. Avoid to have a snack just before going to bed

10. Limit the time you spend in bed. This helps to "strengthen" your sleep: too long periods spent in bed without sleeping will fragment and alleviate your sleep. It is therefore recommended to use your bed only for sleep and sexual activity, not to watch TV, eat, work...

11. Avoid sleeping pills unless your doctor has prescribed some for a reason. Also avoid taking any toxic substances (cannabis, other drugs...) and stimulants (some anti-inflammatory drugs, amphetamines, certain drugs without a prescription or herbal...)[33].

---

[33] When in doubt, ask your doctor or pharmacist.

12. Do not practice intense intellectual work just before bedtime. Set aside a period of calm and relaxation, 30 minutes before going to bed.

13. Do not ruminate your problems of the day when you are in bed. Deep breathing may be associated with relaxation exercises and thaw (see below) just before bed. They can help relieve stress and prepare your mind for a good night's sleep.

14. If you share your room with a pet and you can not sleep, maybe it's time to see that your four legged friend should better go to sleep elsewhere. Animals can cause allergies that affect sleep patterns, and a simple flick of the paw can wake you up. And they make noise at night (grunting, snoring, movements...).

A few more advices:

- Go to bed only when you are tired and ready to sleep.

- If you are unable to fall asleep or to go back to sleep after about thirty minutes, get up and go into another room. Do this as often as necessary. At this point, have a quiet activity (eg drink tea, read an easy reading book...). The need for sleep will return at the next sleep cycle (every 90 minutes).

When you wake up

1. When you awake, get up. If you go back to sleep, you could wake up suddenly during a new cycle.

2. Get up gently. Take time to go back to reality.

3. Expose yourself to light gradually, preferably the light of the day, it helps to regulate your biological clock.

4. Stretch slowly to relax and warm up your muscles.

5. Yawn if you need it, it helps to oxygenate your brain.

6. Have a refreshing shower.

7. Eat a solid and balanced breakfast. It should normally give you 25% of your energy needs for the day.

Of course, these advices are written to be put into practice as part of a light, moderate insomnia. If these techniques are not enough, a consultation with your doctor will be obvious.

Indeed, insomnia can become a true Hell. And the question that settles there is the following: why certain solutions – medicines included – are ineffective? And especially, what do we have to do to resolve the problem?

In fact, with insomnia, the more the person will focus on his confusion of sleep and the more this one deteriorates. Surprising, really? In general, the more you take care efficiently of a problem and the more quickly it disappears. For insomnia, it differs: it is therefore a good indication to say that it is a false problem! When you sleep badly, the aim is obviously to **understand** why you sleep so bad, even before offering a treatment that will only appease the symptom for some time.

To have access to sleep, your organism must unloose all of its tensions, but also the thoughts that are at the origin of these tensions. In fact, the more you get worried at the idea of not sleeping and the less you sleep!

It is therefore more judicious to ask yourself the following question: «*What prevents me from closing the eye?*» rather than to wonder: «*What I am going to take to fall asleep?*».

● **In second time: exercises of relaxation and thaw**:

Such exercises are especially useful when insomnia is occasional or moderate. They aim at diminishing the stress linked to the fact that you don't sleep, and therefore to diminish the tensions of the body and mind. Relaxation allows to the person to be more attentive to the messages that its organism sends him, and to ask the good questions about the origin of its insomnia. Furthermore – an effect which is not negligible – while you train your mind to relax itself, it is not pervaded by the stress of being unable to find sleep.

Two main methods of relaxation can be used in practice: the *autogenous training and the progressive muscular relaxation*:

The autogenous training

The state of relaxation induced by this technique is characterized by :

- A muscular thaw,
- A dilation of blood vessels of the extremities of the arms and legs
- Heart and breathing slowdown
- An abdominal relaxation
- A coolness feeling on the forehead

This state is reached by successive steps, over sessions, working on each of the elements mentioned.

The person moves or lies down (most often) or sit on a chair or a sofa.He will have to focus on both directions (for instance : *«My right arm feels heavy, my left leg is warm, my heart beats slowly and calmly»*), mental representations (for instance : to imagine his right arm as lead or his left leg exposed to sunlight), and bodily sensations that arise (eg. the weight of the right arm, the warmth of the left leg), witnesses the induced changes.

The state of relaxation provided by this technique is acquired in a few months. You can get help at first by a specialist trained in autogenic training before implementing this method at home, in a calm situation.

Progressive muscle relaxation

This form of relaxation is particularly suitable for people who have difficulty surrendering passively to the previous technique, preferring a more active technique. The exercises consist of alternating contraction and relaxation of muscle groups: the subject strongly contracts muscle group and focus on the physical sensations of tension, then release it and gradually relaxes the muscles, focuses similarly on feeling of muscle relaxation.

Successively, different muscle groups are addressed, usually in the following order: hands, arms, forearms, shoulders, neck, jaws, eyes, forehead, back, chest, abdomen, buttocks, legs, calves.

The set of exercises for each muscle group lasts about fifteen minutes. At the beginning, during learning, it is necessary to practice these exercises once or twice a day, alternating contraction and relaxation. Gradually, the person learns to obtain a relaxation of the muscles with less recourse to the initial phase of contraction.

- **If you still cannot sleep: psychotherapy of insomnia - CBT (Cognitivo-Behavior Therapies):**

Behaviour and cognitive therapies (CBT) represent the most widely admitted mode of psychological taking care among all scientific approaches today[34]. CBT are based on techniques that evolve regularly in the course of time, depending on research studies that assess its effectiveness.

These therapies act, as their name points it out, on unadapted behaviours to the common life (example: every evening, Gérard takes a hypnotic in a systematic way before going to bed, by fear of not being able to fall asleep. This "ritual" lasts for more than five years). CBT also acts on thoughts (cognition) associated to these unadapted behaviours (in the case of Gérard: *«If I go to bed without taking my sleeping drug, I am going again to turn myself in my bed during hours, and finally, I won't be able to close the eye all night long»*).

Then, it is about of changing an inadequate behaviour with the intention that the patient improves as soon as possible (maladjusted acts are fought

---

[34] About CBT, read *«For a Fast Recovery – CBT: Instructions»*, edited by LAP LAMBERT Academic Publishing (2005)

and eliminated, adapted activities are favoured and reinforced)[35].
In the case of insomnia, CBT requires that the person gets involved personally in the taking care, and that he takes an active part in his therapy. Under this condition he will be able to find a good quality of sleep.
Then, the techniques used are the following:

 - *The restriction of sleep* that consists in limiting the time passed in bed to the time during which the subject sleeps
 - *The control by the stimulus* that consists in giving a lot of advices to the person aiming at getting a better hygiene of sleep and to avoid any activity that favours awakening
 - *The cognitive therapy*, of which purpose is to change erroneous beliefs that the person has in relation to her confusion of sleep
 - *The education* concerning things to do and things to avoid in a way to spend a good night (avoiding sports practice or drinking coffee before going to bed, for example).

Moreover, we ask the person to assess his sleep throughout CBT, and we use an agenda of sleep (cf. Appendix 3). The sleeper must note every day his hours of bedtime, of waken up, the periods of the night he did not sleep, his naps ...
Let us return a little more in details on techniques used in CBT:

• *The restriction of sleep*:

The restriction of sleep consists in limiting the time passed in bed by the person who sleeps. Generally, when we suffer from insomnia, we have tendency to remain in bed, in a hope to find rest. But finally, we do not manage to sleep better: all that we succeed to do is to get a split sleep and to maintain insomnia. The objective of the restriction of sleep is to give a light state of deprivation of sleep to the person so that he could feel some drowsiness at bedtime. The moment when the person falls asleep in the evening is then favoured, sleep is more regular and deeper. It is therefore more efficient, and of a better quality.
The person in restriction of sleep risks complaining about drowsiness in the course of the day at first; this phenomenon is completely normal, and lasts about 3 weeks. It is important that the therapist takes some time to explain the objective of this method to his patient: I admit, it is never obvious for me to suggest to the person who comes to see me for insomnia to restrain his sleep!
When such method is recommended, it is very important to use the agenda of sleep correcltly to see the evolution of insomnia in the course of time (cf. Appendix 3).

---

[35] About CBT, read «*For a Fast Recovery – CBT: Instructions*», edited by LAP LAMBERT Academic Publishing (2005)

• *Control by stimulus*:

What we call the «ritual of bedtime» (teeth wash, make-up removal, to go to the toilets, having a drink of water, locking the door) is part of activities routine that allows putting you on good conditions to sleep. However, when a person suffers from sleep troubles, these habits become synonymous with apprehension, with anxiety and finally with insomnia.

It is not rare that the insomniac considers his room – in a more or less conscious way – as a place of activation of awakening rather than as a place of rest («*I just have to think to lay down on my bed to be stressed intensely*», said Christophe to me, insomniac for 8 months).

Rituals acquired in reaction to the confusion of sleep (reading in bed, having a nap in the afternoon, to take a hypnotic in the evening) can give some benefits at first, but very quickly, the person is going to realise that he maintains insomnia in long term.

The aim of the control by stimulus is to change these bad habits and these unadapted interpretations by trying to respect certain rules:

Focus : The Control by Stimulus

The stimulus control assumes that the conditioning is an important part of the falling asleep process and of sleep itself, and that we should therefore strengthen the association between the bedroom, the bed, and sleep. We simply have to follow these rules:

1- To go to sleep only when we are tired and ready to sleep.

2- An hour before going to sleep, ceasing all physical and intellectual demanding activities.

3- To use your bed only to sleep: do not read, do not watch TV, do not eat and do not "worry" in your bed. Sexual activity is the only exception to this rule.

4- If you feel unable to fall asleep after 30 minutes, get up and go into another room. Stay awake as long as you wish and then, return to your room to sleep.

5- If you still can not sleep, repeat step 4 as long as necessary.

6- Set the alarm clock and get up at the same time every day, regardless of the duration of sleep the night before. This helps to acquire a constant sleep

---

pattern.

7- Do not have a nap during daytime.

It is important to know that the bad associations are made in the course of time, and that the fact to recreate some more adapted habits requires therefore an uninterrupted and regular effort. You have to persist!

• *Cognitive therapy:*

Cognitive therapy is aimed to allow the insomniac to spot its erroneous beliefs concerning sleep, to envisage alternative hypotheses and to change its behaviour if this one is harmful to a good night of rest.

The person who suffers from insomnia has generally wrong evaluations in relation to sleep: about imaginary fears, unrealistic waitings or about errors of attribution concerning the origin of insomnia, the «way of thinking» of the insomniac is literally maladjusted. This person is going to try everything to find rest, and will change his behavior, little by little, and the way he reasons out. So, if I get worried not to fall asleep at the desired hour, if I rehash the consequences of a sleepless night on the following day, if I tell myself that nothing will change and that I am going again to turn and turn up until early morning, I have big chances not to let myself to go to the arms of Morpheus…

It is necessary to know that worries concerning insomnia do not torment the person only at night. Very often, the insomniac is going to get worried throughout the day about the consequences of the lack of sleep and/or to come. Then, somebody who thinks that his difficulties to fall asleep are about to ruin his life is going to develop some despair which is going to interfere itself with its sleep. The vicious circle is then speeded up…

The fundamental interest of cognitive therapy is to lead the person to question its beliefs in a way to find a more adapted pattern of thinking. Let us take as a concrete model:

Unsuited pattern of thinking	Questioning
«After a bad night's sleep, I know that I am not able to function normally the next day». *«When I'm irritable, anxious or depressed during the day, it is because I slept badly the night before».*	Are these consequences realistic, or exaggerated? Are the negative consequences of a bad night always felt with the same intensity? If it was true, someone who slept less because of good news should be in the same condition the next day, always irritable, anxious or depressed. If irritability and depression are the result of sleep deprivation, it means that people who sleep well are never angry or depressed. Is this true?

• *Education concerning things to do and not to do to spend a good night:*

Here, it is important to give a few simple advices, which raises common sense. Let's have the model of the coffee as an example: the powerful stimulating effects of caffeine take from 30 minutes until one hour to attain their paroxysm, while the organism can take up to eight hours to eliminate this substance. It is necessary to know that caffeine must be used with caution, because it augments heart rate, blood pressure and activity of kidneys. An excessive consumption of coffee during a too long period can create a dependency: the big consumers (more than four cups a day) who abandon their habit can even feel the symptoms of lack (headaches, agitation, tiredness). These symptoms disappear at the end of a few days.

Caffeine is found in coffee, tea, drinks of cola, chocolate, and in various medicines. The fact of use strong doses of caffeine or to take it before going to sleep augments awakenings reduces slow sleep and shortens the period of sleep. Here is what can give a relatively important consumption of coffee (4 cups a day) on sleep:

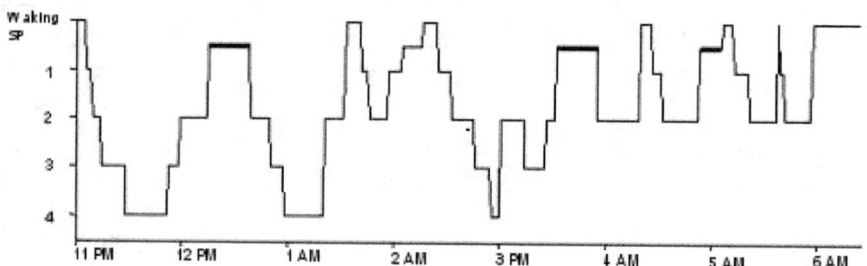

As for cigarette, you must know that nicotine produces two different effects according to its concentration in blood:
- In weak concentration, it is relaxing[36];
- In strong concentration, it thrills. Besides, the smokers take more time than the nonsmokers to fall asleep, and their sleep lasts on average 30 minutes less.

A lively light can also pose problem: the scientists showed that it allows supporting a kind of alertness. Do not forget that light is the main landmark your organism uses to keep your internal rhythms synchronised with the environment.

Physical exercise is also a very good "awakening" activity: to proscribe therefore, as we talk about previously, before bedtime. Finally, the advices concerning the famous nap of the afternoon can be summed up in the chart below:

---

[36] It's the well known cigarette of the evening we smoke before going to bed that allows to relax.

Having a nap: a good or a bad thing?

- It's a bad thing if you are currently insomniac.

- It's bad for you if you try to relax in a noisy place, unproper to relaxation.

- It's bad for you if you extend this nap after around 20 minutes, creating a risk to degrade seriously the quality of your night sleep.

- It's good for you if, after a hearty meal, you really want to sleep and that you can barely stay awaken. In this case, don't try to fight against your need to sleep and give yourself a short nap of 20 minutes. It will help the digest process.

- It's good for you if your position is suitable. Therefore, avoid to sleep if you sit down on an armchair, because your will be at risk to awaken with pains on your back and neck.

- It's good for you if you know from experience that this nap will not interfer with your sleep during the night. Otherwise, avoid having a nap by walking around and breathing some fresh air, in a way to shorten the sleepiness.

As you can see, the therapist adopts generally a much appreciated style by the persons who benefit from the CBT. This style is very different from the classical image of the unruffled, distant, often silent "psychoanalyst" or on the contrary, speaking an esoteric speech. The relation is here:
- Interactive: during a session, the therapist explains, asks questions and answers those of the patient
- Pedagogic and explicit: language is simple (but it does not mean that it is simplistic), explanation is comprehensible
- Collaborative and egalitarian: it consists in determining, in collaboration with the patient, concrete and realistic targets, as well as finding techniques to reach them. Nothing is imposed but everything is displayed, offered and discussed. CBT applied to sleep troubles gives very interesting results; it allows breaking the vicious circle of insomnia, avoiding for the patient to become mindless with the aid of treatments that could be avoided.

o **In last resort: taking a hypnotic**

• *Here is the step followed by your doctor before prescribing a hypnotic:*

Your attending physician is going to have a rather systematic approach in face of the complaint concerning your quality of sleep. At first, he is going to establish a chronicle of your insomnia, he will try to understand the beginning of the process and its evolution. He will have to get, by a careful cross-examination, a description, as definite as possible, of:
- Your working timetables
- The hour when you return home
- The organisation of your flat and of your bedroom
- Your meal times, sleep time, the possible time slot you dedicate yourself for physical exercise
- The quality and durations of your regular sleep (possibly based on a calendar of sleep [cf. Appendix 3])
- Your occupations in case of insomnia
- The quality of your sleep outside home
- The possible taking of tablets or various infusions

The cross-examination of your spouse is interesting, particularly as for your "way" of sleeping (breathing, movements, possible snores...). Of course, your doctor is going to practice a complete clinical examination in search of a medical, neurological or psychiatric reason, at the origin of your insomnia. If it was not already made, he is indeed going to ask you to fill a calendar of sleep, during at least 2 weeks. A polysomnography could be necessary:
- If your doctor suspects an apnea of sleep or another illness that can have serious consequences
- When the reason of insomnia is uncertain
- When the treatment is ineffectual, that it is medicinal or not

In fact, your doctor is going to follow a very definite flowchart, as below[37]:

---

[37] According to Entenmann W, Schwander J, Strub M: *Insomnie chronique : symptôme ou diagnostic ?* Forum Med Suisse 2003; 42: 1000-1007

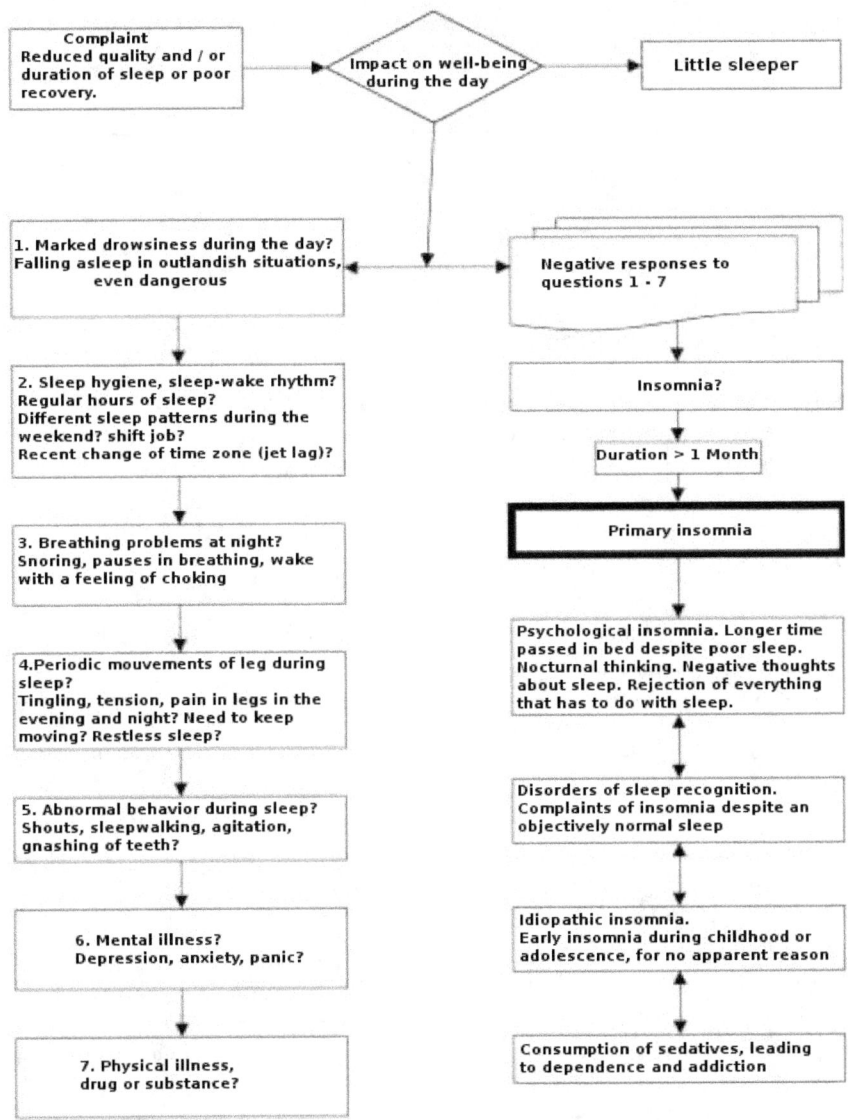

• *Hypnotic or not hypnotic? That's the question...*

Once the doctor put the finger on the nature of the complaint of a person who sleeps badly – or who does not sleep any more – he will have to choose an adapted treatment among the different therapeutic tools he has at his/her disposal. You should not lose of view that as part of sleep troubles, the prescription of hypnotic acts only on symptomatic plan[38]. It is

---

[38] It means that they do not treat the **cause** of insomnia.

important to know that a hypnotic can cause new problems, such as a medicinal dependency itself for example.

Did you know that ?[39]

- Nearly one in ten French consumes hypnotics. In 40% of cases, this decision is regular and lasts for over a month, which is contrary to scientific recommendations.

- In 20-30% of cases, falls among the elderly are associated with taking a hypnotic or sedative (classic case: the person gets up at night to go to the toilet and falls because vigilance is decreased).

- In 2004, the number of boxes of hypnotics and sedatives reimbursed by health insurance increased by 1.7%.

- More than 10 millions of euros are paid annually by the Health Insurance for hypnotics and sedatives.

The hypnotic are defined as «*a group of medicaments that cause a sleep as close as possible as a natural sleep*». The only problem is that it is not just about a natural sleep: the sleeping drug, if it really ease the way to fall asleep, changes the structure of sleep by diminishing the length of the two most important stages, paradoxical sleep and slow deep sleep (stages 3 and 4). Ideally, a hypnotic should have following characteristics:

- Having a quick effect (10 - 15 minutes)
- Being active for at least 5 to 7 hours
- Preserving sleep architecture, without loss of deep sleep and / or REM sleep
- Creating no respiratory problems, memory disorders
- Having no interaction with other medicines, or with alcohol
- Creating no dependency
- Requiring no gradual increase in doses to maintain its effectiveness
- Preserving alertness throughout the day

Unfortunately, such ideal sleeping drug does not exist! Consumption of

---

[39] Source : CNAMTS (National fund of health insurance for employees) – Ipsos Survey, January 2005

hypnotic must therefore never become a habit, under no circumstances: they indeed cause a dependency, when you stop the treatment, with phenomenon of weaning (phenomenon of lack). You can't take this type of medication without the opinion of your doctor who, it is necessary to know it, will be able to prescribe you some, only for a length of **a month** at the farthest (sometimes less). In any case, it is still better to discern the precise reason of insomnia that it is frequently easy to treat without sleeping drugs.

France holds the record of use of sleeping pills: every day, we take about ten million of drugs against insomnia! Several categories exist, which it is not necessary to itemise here. The most known category (and the most damaging) is that of benzodiazepines.

Here is a small summary picture:

Prescription Time	International Generic Denomination
4 WEEKS	Dipotassic Clorazepate
	Estazolam
	Loprazolam
	Lormetazépam
	Meprobamate
	Nitrazepam
	Témazepam
	Zopiclone
	Zolpidem
2 WEEKS	Triazolam
2 WEEKS but fractionation on 7 days	Flunitrazépam

(Acoording to the French Agency for Sanitary Safety of Health Products)

When they are prescribed during limited time and with parsimony, the hypnotic can render a great service to the insomniac, but it is well necessary to know the risks:

 - For the great majority of them, they are at the origin of still present sedative effects in the morning and during the waking: therefore, they diminish concentration, or even intellectual and physical capacities of the person

 - Their effects – particularly as for benzodiazépines – diminish with time, which draws a habituation[40] that can be at the origin of a vicious circle of which it is then very difficult to get rid:

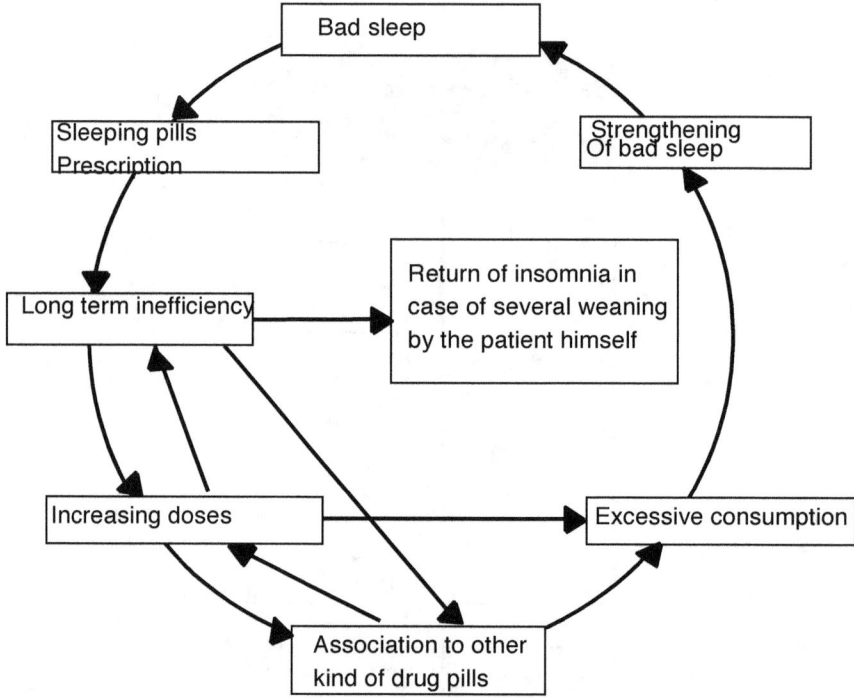

The bounce back of insomnia during trials of violent cessation reinforces the idea of not being able to sleep without hypnotic. The most obvious result of this escalation is a raised disorganisation of sleeping that becomes distinctly worse than before all kind of treatment. From this position, there is only one solution that comes: a very progressive weaning (under the help of a strong support by the medicated doctor): one product at once, with

---

[40] Necessity to increase the dose to get the same effect.

reduction to a half dose – or even to a quarter of dose – by steps of 8 to 10 days. Complete weaning sometimes requires more than three months. Thus, in many of case, it is still better to avoid an uninterrupted treatment, but to prefer a discontinuous treatment like a tablet the first night, half tablet second night, a quarter the third and anything more for the rest of the week. Such therapeutic diagram prevents a «conditioned strengthening» of insomnia due to the succession of bad nights, and the long-term effectiveness of the hypnotic is kept while allowing to "program" a few good nights a week.

In light of these possible problems, it is easy to make some warning. And please, if you had to keep only one thing of this work, be sure it is the following paragraph:

- A hypnotic must be used only after a consultation to your medicated doctor, and only on prescription. Be wary of «good advice» of auntie Lucienne or of Madam Durand, the next-door neighbour (*«my husband did not sleep well last summer, then his doctor recommended him this medicine. You should try... I still have some tablets»*)

- Children must be the most possible preserved from these substances (to avoid therefore the drops of a sleeping drug in the nursing bottle[41] when baby have his teeth!)

- The association of alcohol and hypnotic is strictly inadvisable (vital risk is then in jeopardy, the person could be victim of an acute respiratory insufficiency)

- The length of the hypnotic treatment must be limited **to less of a month**[42]

- The cessation of the treatment must be progressive, and be made according to a protocol established by the medicated doctor

- The taking of the medicine must take place «in last resort». Let us have a concrete model as example. Michel finds it difficult to sleep; he goes to sleep habitually at 11 pm, and as he is afraid of being inable to find sleep, he takes his hypnotic at 10:30 pm. By doing like this, he has all chances to become dependent to his treatment: the day he will not take his sleeping drug, he will be so much worried at the idea of not falling asleep that he will really not find sleep![43] The ideal thing to do is to go about things in the following

---

[41] It can even be drops of pastis or strong alcohol, which sedative qualities were once touted by our grandmothers!

[42] Just in case, ask someone you know he takes a sleeping drug for how long he consummes this kind of medicine: generally, it might be for many years!

[43] In addition, upon reflection, this approach is totally meaningless: Michel "takes a sleep medication, in case he would not sleep!"

way: Michel goes to sleep at 11 pm; puts his hypnotic on his night table and gives himself untill midnight to fall asleep. If he does not sleep at midnight, then he will take his medicine. In this second scenario, the person is reassured, and generally, he falls asleep without the help of a treatment.

Side effects of sleeping tablets are not systematic, but they can have a significant impact on the quality of the day to come: though waking, nausea and headaches in the rising, tendency to drowsiness throughout the morning, fall of performances at work, are some examples of the discomforts that can be felt the day after the taking of a sleeping drug. When a benzodiazepine is used, memory disturbances can happen (some sleeping drugs are besides sadly famous in the case of rapes with inability to remember whatever it was, the girls having been doped without knowing it by these substances in nightclubs).

All benzodiazépines has four properties together:
- An anxiolytic effect, "that relieves distress": benzodiazepines diminishe emotional tensions and appease the expressions of anxiety
- A hypnotic effect: benzodiazepines favours sleep by augmenting its length; they reduce nocturnal awakenings and improve the time needed to fall asleep. But the sleep created leads to modifications of its structure; it is not therefore a physiological sleep
- An antiepileptic effect: this property allows using benzodiazepines as a treatment of epilepsy
- A muscular relaxant effect

Finally, it is necessary to keep in mind that benzodiazepines increases apnea of sleep (thus, the necessity, I repeat it, not to neglect the check-up performed by your medicated doctor).

During a violent cessation, we see a quick rebound of insomnia, headaches, of an important anxiety, muscular pain, and sometimes, a fretfullness, an agitation, or even confusion. More unusually, it is possible to note shakings, sensory hallucinatory phenomena (visual, gustatory, auditory or olfactory), or even of convulsions.

Then, in summary, if you take a sleeping drug, follow this practical advice:

1. Learn to know your medicine

- What is its exact name?

- How many pills do you have to take by day?

- How many days should you take this medication?

- Can you drive or use mechanical tools?

- Can you still drink alcoholic beverages?

2. Prefer lower dosages

- Do not ask something to stun to your doctor.

- Do not take 2 pills if your doctor prescribe 1 pill in the evening.

3. Do not drink alcohol with your medication

- Even a small quantity of alcohol can be enough to knock you off, to make you weak and   vulnerable.

- You may suffer from a faintness, or even die (by acute respiratory failure).

4. Inform your doctor of every kind of medication you take

- Some substances associated with hypnotics can cause very serious side effects.

5. Do not hesitate to see your doctor if you feel unpleasant effects or if the prescribed hypnotic did not have the desired effect

- Do not change the treatment that has been prescribed to you by your own.

6. Do not take sleepin drugs for more than a week, unless your doctor recommend it

- Contrary to what one might think, sleeping pills over a long period can cause sleep disorders.

7. Consult your doctor if you decide to stop your hypnotic

- If you take a hypnotic for a short time and that you stop suddenly, you may have trouble sleeping, feeling nervous or being irritable for a few days.

- If you take a hypnotic for a long time and that you stop suddenly, you may be feel very sick and being a victim of a true withdrawal syndrome.

8. Never borrow a hypnotic to someone (even if it is your spouse) and never share yours

- A medicine suitable to a parent, a friend or neighbor should not necessarily be appropriate to you, or even can be dangerous for you.

9. Limit the use of hypnotic to the periods of real insomnia

- It means that sleep disorder is installed for several weeks, and it has no known cause that can be treated (see DSM IV criteria).

CONCLUSION

In our modern society, men and women get up early, they go late to sleep and have sometimes, in many cases, to take sleeping drugs to fall asleep easily, unaware of the risks of dependency and of familiarisation these medicines can hazard.

How is it possible to highlight a lack of sleep? In fact, it is very simple: if you remain in bed till noon during the weekend while habitually you go to do some sports at 9 am, or if you wake up every day of the week completely exhausted, there are irrefutably a few signals that have to warn you: your nights are too short, indeed not refreshing. If your body and mind feel bad, it is often the result of a lack of sleep.

What I would like that you remember from this work is that the most important thing is to avoid missing a trouble of sleep, and especially as it is necessary to treat the true origin of the problem. Here is an example of approach that orientated a doctor to the precise origin of insomnia. He will allow you to see that you should not only become attached to the following symptom: «*I do not sleep well*».

Franck, a 22 years-old young man, suffers from insomnia for about six months. He is not seriously concerned about this problem, until he falls asleep when he was driving his car and almost killed himself on the road. Then, he went to see his medicated doctor, and spoke to him about his difficulties: he finds it difficult to fall asleep, wakes up early in the morning and has tendency to doze off several times during the day. By deepening the interview a bit, the practitioner highlights a true nervous breakdown, which was finally resolved in a few months with the help of an adapted antidepressant treatment linked to a psychotherapy (psychological, professional and emotional problems seemed to have thrown confusion).

A few months later, the young man managed to deal a bit better with his loving relation and finally decided of a professional reorientation. This move helped him to discover its true value and his own capacities, what allows him to find confidence in himself and to assert himself in his personal life. He walked along especially at the level of his identity, top the risk of being more and more himself. Little by little, he gained a lot of satisfaction.

Globally, the development of this young man was affected in a very positive way by the taking care. Imagine what would have arrived at short and long-term if it had continued to minimise his problem of insomnia? Or else, if he had made hush up by a simple hypnotic treatment?

And then, it is about a case where a very specific origin – a depression – is highlighted. Often, a simple defect of the hygiene of sleep will lead to rebel insomnia. Bad habits are developed, we let us have an inappropriate rhythm to our daily life, and progressively, we fall over the Hell of sleepless nights …

What I hope to have given in the course of these some chapters to you, is a practical knowledge of sleep and its mechanisms – because to understand better «how it works» permits to avoid some errors – linked to easy and clear advice to be applied; they allow you to sleep better. By respecting these simple rules, you should, without serious difficulty, find the way to the Land of Dreams more quickly.

To finish, I let you contemplate this sentence of Pierre Billon: «*Sleep is the sovereign river of life, and the dream its alluvium*».

Have a good night !

APPENDIX 1 : EPWORTH SCALE FOR THE VALUATION OF DROWSINESS

In these 8 following circumstances,
Are you at risk of falling asleep during the day?

- If this risk is nonexistent, check 0
- If this risk is negligible, check 1
- If this risk is quite moderated, check 2
- If this risk is important, check 3

Example: If the risk of falling asleep "sat by reading a book or a newspaper" is moderated, check 2

	Answer			
1. Sat when reading a book or a newspaper	0	1	2	3
2. When you watch television	0	1	2	3
3. Sat, inactive, in a public place (cinema, theater, waiting room)	0	1	2	3
4. If you are a passenger in a car during an hour trip	0	1	2	3
5. Lying down after lunch, when situation permits	0	1	2	3
6. Sat down, talking with someone	0	1	2	3
7. Sat down, after a lunch, without alcoholic beverage	0	1	2	3
8. Driving you car, during a stop of the traffic for a few minutes	0	1	2	3
Total				

If your score is up to 15, you are really an "over dozy" person. You should talk about that problem with your doctor.

APPENDIX 2 : QUIZ – ARE YOU MORE ABOUT GOING LATE TO BED IN THE EVENING OR DO YOU WAKE UP EARLY IN THE MORNING ?

(Test proposed on the Website http://sommeil.univ-lyon1.fr/index_f.html)

Score

1 – When do you prefer to wake up?

Between 5 and 6 am	5 points
Between 6 and 7:15 am	4 points
Between 7:15 and 9:45 am	3 points
Between 9:45 and 11 am	2 points
Between 11 and 12 am	1 point

2 – When do you prefer to go to sleep?

Between 8 and 9:30 pm	5 points
Between 9 :30 and 10:45 pm	4 points
Between 10:45 pm and 00:45 am	3 points
Between 00:45 and 2 am	2 points
Between 2 and 3 am	1 point

3 – To wake up early, do you need a clock-radio?

Not at all	4 points
Rather not	3 points
Rather yes	2 points
Absolutely	1 point

4 – For you, to wake up early is:

Very tiresome	1 point
Tiresome	2 points
Rather easy	3 points
Very easy	4 points

5 – During the first half hour of the awaken time, you are:

Asleep	1 point
Lightly awaken	2 points
Quite well awaken	3 points
Totally awaken	4 points

6 – Your hunger, during the first half hour of the day is:

Nonexistent	1 point
Poor	2 points
Rather important	3 points
Very important	4 points

7 – During the first half hour of the day, you feel:

Very tired	1 point
Rather tired	2 points
Rather well rested	3 points
Completely rested	4 points

8 – If you have nothing to do the next day, you are going to sleep:

Not even later	4 points
Less than an hour later	3 points
Between 1 and 2 hours later	2 points
More than 2 hours later	1 point

9 – At night, you feel tired and you want to go to sleep:

Between 8 and 9 pm	5 points
Between 9 and 10:15 pm	4 points
Between 10:15 pm and 0:30 am	3 points
Between 0:30 and 1:45 am	2 points
Between 1:45 and 3 am	1 point

10 – If you exercise twice a week between 7:00 and 8:00, you feel:

In a good shape	4 points
Rather in a good shape	3 points
Rather in a bad shape	2 points
In a very bad shape	1 point

11 – When do you prefer to face a tiring intellectual test?

Between 8 and 10 am	6 points
Between 11 am and 1 pm	4 points
Between 3 and 5 pm	2 points
Between 7 and 9 pm	0 point

12 – If you went to bed after 11 pm, the next day you feel:

Not tired at all	0 points
A bit tired	2 points
Rather tired	3 points
Very tired	5 points

13 – If you are on duty between 4 and 6 in the morning:

You are going to sleep only after your work time	1 point
You have a nap before and you go to sleep thereafter	2 points
You sleep the much as you can before and you have a nap thereafter	3 points
You sleep before and you don't go to sleep thereafter	4 points

14 – To do a tiring work, you will do it:

Between 8 and 10 am	4 points
Between 11 am and 1 pm	3 points
Between 3 and 5 pm	2 points
Between 7 and 9 pm	1 point

15 – Practicing a tiring sport between 10 and 11 am twice a week, after your exercices, you feel:

In a good shape	1 point
In a relative good shape	2 points
Rather in a bad shape	3 points
In a very bad shape	4 points

16 – If you should have to choose an hour to begin a work of 5 hours long, you should choose:

Between 4 and 8 am	5 points
Centered around 8 am	4 points
Between 9 am and 1 pm	3 points
Between 1 pm and 5 pm	2 points
Between 5 and 10 pm	1 point

17 – When you are going to sleep late, the morning after you wake up at:

On time, without going back to sleep	4 points
On time, but feeling sleepy a moment after	3 points
On time, but you go back to sleep	2 points
Later than usual	1 point

18 – When do you feel in your best shape?

Between 4 and 7 am	5 points
Between 7 and 9 am	4 points
Between 10 am and 5 pm	3 points
Between 5 pm and 10 pm	2 points
Between 10 pm and 4 am	1 point

Total   **points**

If you sum:

More than 70 points: You are really an early riser.
Between 59 and 69 points: Rather an early person.
Between 42 and 58 points: In a medium situation.
Between 31 and 41 points: Rather an evening person.

More than 30 points: You are really an evening person.

APPENDIX 3 : AGENDA OF SLEEP

(Offered by the Website http://www.sommeil-mg.net/accueil.php)

This agenda is intended to give the maximum of information on your rest and activity schedule. It is a bit tiring job, but it can lead to establish a diagnosis, provided that the information you bring is reliable and accurate.

Instructions of use:
For every period of 24 hours, you are going to note:
> - The hour of bedtime and wake up, by vertical arrows ↑ and ↓
> - The periods of the night when you think you weren't sleeping:
> - Naps.

It is important to signal by letters - codes some elements of your days and nights:
> - W: each time you are going to urinate or to drink (especially during the night)
> - P: when you have an important physical activity
> - Fr: if you have bouts of tiredness (without sleeping).

Use the space "comments" to point out a possible take of medicines, notable events, bouts of drowsiness, etc.
Finally, you are going to give a note from 1 to 5 to judge your nights, the highest note describing a maximum satisfaction.

Note: For convenience of reading, the day starts at midday. The agenda is envisaged for 15 days (D1 to D15).

Jerome PALAZZOLO

Wakening / Sleep Agenda

First name : ....   Name : ....

From ....To ....   Date of Birth : ....

	12pm 1pm 2pm 3pm 4pm 5pm 6pm 7pm 8pm 9pm 10pm 11pm 12pm 1am 2am 3am 4am 5am 6am 7am 8am 9am 10am 11am 12am	Day	Night	COMMENTS
D 1				
D 2				
D 3				
D 4				
D 5				
D 6				
D 7				
D 8				
D 9				
D 10				
D 11				
D 12				
D 13				
D 14				
D 15				

12pm 1pm 2pm 3pm 4pm 5pm 6pm 7pm 8pm 9pm 10pm 11pm 12pm 1am 2am 3am 4am 5am 6am 7am 8am 9am 10am 11am 12am

APPENDIX 4 – EXAMPLE OF INFORMATION ON INSOMNIA, FOR THE GENERAL PUBLIC

The Insomnia
To sleep well at night

What is the cause of insomnia?

Many people suffer from insomnia or sleep disorders. Some can not fall asleep, others wake up during the night and no longer find sleep, and others wake up very early in the morning.

Insomnia is not a disease. This is a way the body takes to say that something is wrong. The causes of insomnia are many: stress, over consumption of caffeine, depression, changes in work schedule and pain associated with certain medical problems, such as arthritis.

Is insomnia a serious problem?

Insomnia can be a serious problem. 30% to 40% of adults suffer from certain forms of insomnia year round. Insomnia increases with age and is more common in women. It may lessen your ability to work and cause anxiety or tension. People who suffer from insomnia often feel tired, depressed and irritable and have difficulty concentrating. Insomnia may be responsible for drowsiness in car and labor accidents and other risks of health problems.

How many hours of sleep do I need?

Most adults need about eight hours of sleep each night. You know you've slept enough if you do not want to sleep during the day. For some people, six hours is enough. Others need ten hours of sleep. Sleep patterns change with age. For example, seniors take a nap during the day and sleep less at night. In general, your sleep needs in adulthood will remain essentially the same.

How my doctor can find the cause of my insomnia?

Your family doctor may ask, to you and your spouse (if possible), some questions to identify the cause of your insomnia. He will ask about your habits (hours of bedtime and wake up, for example), medications you take, the amount of caffeine, alcohol and tobacco you consume.

Your doctor will also search for the circumstances that could disrupt your life and therefore your sleep. These issues may affect your work and personal relationships.

He will ask you how long you have insomnia, if you experience pain, for example if you have arthritis if you snore or if you have sudden movements of the legs during sleep.

If these questions do not suffice to identify the cause of your insomnia, your doctor may recommend that you keep a journal of your sleep habits. This journal will help you specify your bedtime, the time it takes to fall asleep, the number of times you wake up during the night, the time when you wake up in the morning and the quality of your sleep.

How to treat insomnia?

Sometimes the treatment of insomnia is very simple. Often insomnia disappears by itself when you have identified the cause and that appropriate changes were made. The important thing is to find the cause and to intervene directly on it.

If your insomnia is related to stress, you may need to reduce its level or learn to control it. If you experience a depressive episode, your family doctor may advise you to consult a psychotherapist or to take a medication.

Sleeping pills, do they help?

Hypnotics (sleeping pills) are sometimes useful, but they can also aggravate insomnia. They provide only temporary relief and do not cure anything. Their use should not exceed one or two weeks. Taken regularly, they can cause rebound insomnia. This type of insomnia occurs when a person stops taking sleeping pills and insomnia starts over again. So instead of treating insomnia, sleeping pills may be the cause.

Medicines that you buy over the counter are often ineffective. As for drugs obtained on prescription, they can transform your normal sleep and make you feel drowsy and dizzy in the morning. In addition, sleeping pills lose their effectiveness over time, it is necessary to increase the dosage. This is why you should not take sleeping pills for long periods.

Sleeping pills can be dangerous if your insomnia is caused by a health problem. Your doctor can tell you if they are safe and useful in your case.

How to improve my sleep habits?

Here are some tips to help you sleep better.

- Go to bed and get up at the same time every day, even if you do not get enough sleep the night before. Thus, your body will get used to sleep at night.
- Follow the same routine every night before going to bed to prepare your body to sleep in a better way. Either try to take a hot bath, read or do an activity that promotes relaxation every night before going to bed. You will soon make the connection between these activities and sleep, which will help you sleep.
- Reserve the bedroom for sleep. Avoid eating, phoning or watching TV in bed.
- Your bedroom should be quiet and dark. If noise bothers you, use a fan or take hearing protection. You may also install blinds or drapes on windows, or to hide the eyes.
- Do not try to force yourself to sleep. The more you try, the more it can be difficult to fall asleep. Do not watch the clock. Turn the dial in a way that you can't have a look on time.
- It can be frustrating to be lying while being unable to fall asleep. If you are still awake after 30 minutes, get up and go into another room. Relax in a chair for 20 minutes before returning to bed. Repeat this action as many times as necessary.

Suggestions to improve sleep

- Exercise more often, but not during the hours before bedtime.
- Once in bed, do not dwell on your worries. Think about it another time. For example, take 30 minutes after dinner to write down your concerns and possible solutions.
- Take a light snack before bed but do not overeat. A glass of warm milk or crackers with a piece of cheese is enough.
- Do not have a nap in the afternoon if you think it will prevent you from sleeping at night.

This brochure gives you an overview of the topic and may not apply to all cases. To determine if this brochure is for you and for more information on this topic, please consult your family doctor.

This material received a favorable opinion from the CFPC Committee charged with revising the educational materials for patients.
The College of Family Physicians of Canada, 2630 Skymark Avenue, Mississauga (Ontario) L4W 5A4.

Jerome PALAZZOLO

APPENDIX 5 : THEY WROTE…

Normal sleep and its disturbances was always an important source of inspiration for many authors. Here are some quotations I let you meditate…

To see so many people who sleep and fall asleep in night, I will end up, it is fatal, to fall asleep as well.
Barbara

Dreams were created so that we do not get bored during sleep.
Francis Blanche

Never believe straightaway in the misfortune of men. Ask them only if they can still sleep? If they can, everything goes well. This is enough.
Louis-Ferdinand Céline

My torment is to be able to sleep. If I had always slept well, I would have never written a line.
Louis-Ferdinand Céline

It's impossible to love life when it's not possible to sleep.
Emile-Michel Cioran

Even more than time, sleep is the antidote of sorrow. Insomnia, on the other hand, grows on the slightest vexation and converts it into a blow of fate; it watches on our wounds and prevents them from perishing.
Emile-Michel Cioran

Living is an illness, of which sleep relieves us every sixteen hours; it's a palliative: death is the only cure.
Chamfort

It is necessary to say the rosary when we don't sleep and not add the night to the day for which it has his own mischief.
Paul Claudel

Sleep is not any more a sure place.
Jean Cocteau

Suffering from insomnia, I would well exchange a mattress of feather for a sleep of lead.
Pierre Dac

To be happy, we need to sleep a lot and to defecate well. The insomniac and his first cousin, the constipated, are the damned souls of the earth.
Frederic Dard

There is no pain that sleep can't defeat.
Honoré de Balzac

The surprising transformation of sleep makes us equal to the Gods.
Robert Desnos

Sleep is a reward for some, a suffering for others. For all, it is a sanction.
Isidore Ducasse

I don't sleep for a long time, but I sleep fast.
Albert Einstein

We have the proof that it is always when we get up that we want to sleep. So, we should wait to gets up to lie down!
Georges Feydeau

Neither tempered by the light, nor curbed by the external world, the thought of the insomniac develops its branches pleasantly and displays them up to the huge, the monstrous, into the night.
André Gide

The child had chosen the surest mode of escape in this world. He slept.
Jean Giraudoux

Did you point out that, whatever the noise that awakens you, it ceases as soon as you are awakened?
Sacha Guitry

Her sleep was, for the most, what she had the deepest.
Sacha Guitry

Better is a quiet conscience than a prosper destiny. I prefer a good sleep than a good bed.
Victor Hugo

Sleep - For some, is a way to become rich. Drama is the number of insomniacs.
Jean-François Kahn
Isn't it hard to think that some writers dedicate long nights to soporific works and give to unknowns some beneficial effect that they lose themselves?
Paul Masson

Too much sleep gives headaches. And the excess of sleep is like to live as an animal.
Moliere

Poor man! I don't like, says God, the man who does not sleep.
Charles Péguy

A man who sleeps holds the thread of the hours around him, the order of the years and of the worlds.
Marcel Proust

Jerome PALAZZOLO

TO KNOW MORE…

Benoit O, Foret J: *Le sommeil humain.* Masson, Paris, 1991

Benoit O, Goldenberg F: *Explorations du sommeil et de la vigilance chez l'adulte.* EM Inter, Paris, 1997

Benoit O: *Physiologie du sommeil.* Masson, Paris, 1984

Billiard M: *Le sommeil normal et pathologique.* Masson, Paris, 1998

Billiard M: *Sommeil et éveil. De la théorie… à la pratique.* Editions Espaces 34, Paris, 1997

Borbely A: *Les secrets du sommeil.* Belfond, Paris, 1985

Brenot P: *Les mots du sommeil.* PUF, Paris, 1989

Chneiweiss L: *Dormir n'est plus un rêve.* Albin Michel, Paris, 1993

De Leersnyders H: *L'enfant et son sommeil.* Robert Lafon, Paris, 1998

Dement WC, Vaughan C: *Avoir un bon sommeil.* Odile Jacob, Paris, 2000

Étevenon P: *Du rêve à l'éveil.* Albin Michel, Paris, 1987

Fleury B, Hausser-Haw C, Bacqué MF: *Ronflements et apnées du sommeil.* Odile Jacob, Paris, 1998

Gaillard JM: *Le sommeil, ses mécanismes et ses troubles.* Doin, Paris, 1990

Gaillard JM: *L'insomnie.* Flammarion, Paris, 1993

Garma L: *Clinique de l'insomnie.* PUF, Paris, 1994

Gay M: *Sous les ailes du sommeil.* Editions Dervy, Paris, 1999

Gentils R: *Les troubles du sommeil.* Editions Mango Pratique, Paris, 2002

Jouvet M, Gessain M: *Le grenier des rêves.* Odile Jacob, Paris, 1997

Jouvet M: *Le château des songes.* Odile Jacob, Paris, 1992

Jouvet M: *Le sommeil et le rêve.* Odile Jacob, Paris, 1992

Lavie P: *Le monde du sommeil.* Odile Jacob, Paris, 1996

Lecendreux M: *Réponses à 100 questions sur le sommeil.* Solar, Paris, 2002

Léger D: *Troubles du sommeil.* Doin, Paris, 2001

Léger D: *Le sommeil roi.* First Editions, Paris, 1998

Manceaux M: *Éloge de l'insomnie.* Hachette, Paris, 1985

Morin CM: *Vaincre les ennemis du sommeil.* Marabout, Paris, 2000

Nemet-Pier L: *Moi, la nuit je fais jamais dodo.* Fleurus, Paris, 2000

Ohayon M: *Dis-moi comment tu dors.* Les Empêcheurs de Penser en Rond, Paris, 1997

Palazzolo J, Roure L: *Ecarts de conduite - Sécurité routière et psychopathologie.* Ellipses, Collection Vivre et Comprendre, Paris, 2004

Renaud A, Savier L: *Dormir, l'énigme de chaque nuit.* Autrement, Paris, 1991

Royant-Parola S: *Comment retrouver le sommeil par soi-même.* Odile Jacob, Paris, 2002

Royant-Parola S: *Le bon sommeil.* Hermann, Paris, 1988

Shapiro CM: *ABC des troubles du sommeil.* Maloine, Paris, 1996

Thirion M, Challamal MJ: *Le sommeil, le rêve et l'enfant.* Albin Michel, Paris, 2002

Thirion M, Challamel MJ: *Le sommeil, le rêve et l'enfant.* Albin Michel, Paris, 1995

Valatx JL: *Les troubles du sommeil.* Arnaud Franel Editions, Paris, 2001

Vecchierini MF: *Le guide du sommeil.* John Libbey Eurotext, Paris, 1997

...AND EVEN MORE

Autret A, Gaillard P: *Sommeil et pathologie de l'encéphale.* Rapport de Neurologie, LXXXVIIIème session du Congrès de Psychiatrie et de Neurologie de Langue Française, Masson, Paris, 1990

Durst P, Palazzolo J, Peyrelong JP, Berger M, Chalabreysse M, Billiard M, Vialle A: *Méthadone et syndrome d'apnées du sommeil.* The Canadian Journal of Psychiatry 2005; 50(3): 153-158

Ferreri M: *Le sommeil et ses troubles en psychiatrie.* Revue des Sciences Médicales 1989; 3: 69-79

Palazzolo J, Chabannes JP: *A propos des troubles du sommeil en psychiatrie.* Le Journal de Nervure 2003; 16(5): 1-3

Palazzolo J, Chabannes JP: *Troubles du sommeil et pathologie psychiatrique : état des lieux.* Nervure 2002; 15(7): 5-10

Palazzolo J: *Troubles du sommeil et prescription d'hypnotiques : données actuelles et perspectives.* Nervure 2001; 14(6): 13-17

Palazzolo J: *Neurobiologie des fonctions du sommeil et de ses troubles. Application à la clinique psychiatrique.* Annales de Psychiatrie 2000; 15: 50-57

Palazzolo J, Chabannes JP: *À propos de l'étude des fonctions du sommeil en psychiatrie.* Nervure 1999; 12(8): 7-10

Royant-Parola S: *Sommeil et affections psychiatriques : l'anxieux, le névrosé, le déprimé, le maniaque, etc.* In: Troubles du sommeil et de la vigilance en pratique quotidienne, Laboratoires Upjohn, 63-67

Science et Vie 1993; 185 (n° Hors Série)

Touchon J: *Les troubles du sommeil dépendant des maladies psychiatriques dans la classification internationale des troubles du sommeil.* Neuro-Psy 1991; 6(7): 337-344

Jerome PALAZZOLO

USEFULL ADDRESSES

● **Association nationale de PROmotion des connaissances sur le SOMmeil (PROSOM) :**

Adresse : Hôpital de l'Hôtel-Dieu, porte 17
1, place de l'Hôpital
69288 Lyon cedex 02

Phone : +33 4 78 42 10 77

Website : http://sommeil.univ-lyon1.fr/PROSOM

The PROSOM association, partner of the National Institute of Prevention and Education for Health (INPES) and of the Institute of Sleep and Alertness (ISV), regroups scientists, training officers and actors on the ground for cooperations, exchanges and common creations in a way to set up actions of sensitisation or of education on sleep, alertness and rhythms of life.

PROSOM assures the organisation and animation of trainings, meetings, conferences, debates, production and broadcasting of pedagogic support adapted to different publics, as well as methodological expertises.

On the Internet, you will find site dates and places of seminars of training offered by PROSOM, of pedagogic booklets and explicative diaporamas.

• Association Sommeil et Santé :

Adresse : Sommeil et Santé
            BP 28
            92362 Meudon-la-Forêt Cedex
Website : http://www.sommeilsante.asso.fr
The *Sommeil et Santé* Association gathers the patients, the doctors, and nursing staff as well as the healthy persons in purpose:
- To bring the recognition of the pathology of sleep as a priority of public health
- To inform the public of the existence and especially of the gravity of sleep disturbances, but also about the possibility to treat and even to cure them
- To relieve the action of centres or laboratories of sleep to the general practitioners, company works doctors, school doctors, male and female nurses
- To obtain the recognition of the specificity of sleep disturbances from the authorities and the set up of an appropriate legislation
- To organise meetings between persons attained by sleep disturbances to allow them to exchange about their experiments
- To help his members to find answers to their problems (information, explanation, specialists' addresses), and to make relations with social security and administration easier for them.
A series of tests is offered on the site, tests allowing you to suspect a possible insomnia, drowsiness, narcolepsy, or even an apnea of sleep if your nights are not peaceful.
A FAQ can be used to approach a particular subject and to discuss it with other internauts.

• Institut du Sommeil et de la Vigilance (ISV) :

Website : http://www.institut-sommeil-vigilance.com
This very nice site to visit offers several small syntheses allowing to understand better what is alertness, sleep and its disturbances. Do not hesitate to go to visit the exhibition on sleep offered by the Home of Solenn: By taking you for a walk in a virtual environment, you will be able to get all information necessary for a better apprehension of affections that can spoil you at night.

• Je ronfle, moi ?

Website : http://site.voila.fr/je_ronfle
This site, created by a nurse who works within a laboratory of sleep, offers many information concerning nocturnal snores and apnea of sleep. On this address, you can find some answers to such basic questions – but however

fundamental – as:
- Is apnea of sleep dangerous for health?
- Is it possible to snore without suffering inevitably from a syndrome of apnea of sleep?
- Is the surgical treatment of apnea of sleep simple?
- My nose is always blocked, or I have problems of nasal partition: will I be able to support a mask all night in case of apnea of sleep?
- Where to find a center of examination of sleep?
- Do I have to be hospitalized to perform my examination of sleep?

● La grande aventure du sommeil :

Website :http://www.sommeil.org
Created on the initiative of the Province of Luxembourg, this very didactic site offers concrete explanation on the normal and pathological sleep of the child from 7 to 12 years old. Information is at the same time intended for the parents (cf. The sleep of children explained to the adults) and to the children (cf. The sleep of children explained to children). Practical advices are given, allowing to avoid some errors that can be at the origin of the insomnia of the child.

● Réseau Morphée :

Adresse : 2 Grande Rue
                92380 Garches
Website :http://www.reseau-morphee.org
Le réseau Morphée is a network of management of chronic sleep disturbances: Insomnia, excessive drowsiness, apnea of sleep, somnambulism, narcolepsy... it regroups various professionals of health (doctors, nurses, physical therapists, psychologists, psychomotility therapists, nurses at home), of which objective is to work together to take care of the patients in a much better way. The network aims to an optimization of the patient management by a close collaboration of the city doctors and with hospital structures.
The site offers clear explanations concerning sleep disturbances, direct access to your medical records if you are taken care by network, as well as a blog about sleep.

● **Société Française de Recherche sur le Sommeil :**

Adresse : Unité d'Hypnologie
    Hôpital Neurologique
    69677 Bron cedex

Phone : +33 4 72 35 71 68

Website : http://sommeil.univ-lyon1.fr/sfrs

The French Research society on Sleep has as purposes:

- To ease the exchanges about Scientific Information and to help in personal contact between the researchers in the field of physiology and of pathology of sleep
- To create and to encourage research in these domains
- To define and to support the best criteria of value for equipment, techniques and methods, for training and education of the medical staff and paramedic
- To defend the specificity of units of sleep in their mode of functioning next to authorities, and the profile of the persons they employ
- To help out and to give its advice to any centres, institutions, persons wanting to study the physiology of sleep or to take care of patients suffering from sleep disturbances.

The Internet site offers much information on the different sleep disturbances, trainings and congresses to come. Bibliographic references can be consulted.

The French Research society on Sleep publishes a magazine called *Sleep and alertness*, accessible online.